Martial Rose Library

The Religious Life of Dress

Previously published in the Series

Helen Bradley Foster, *'New Raiments of Self': African American Clothing in the Antebellum South*
Claudine Griggs, *S/he: Changing Sex and Changing Clothes*
Michaele Thurgood Haynes, *Dressing Up Debutantes: Pageantry and Glitz in Texas*
Anne Brydon and Sandra Niessen, *Consuming Fashion: Adorning the Transnational Body*
Dani Cavallaro and Alexandra Warwick, *Fashioning the Frame: Boundaries, Dress and the Body*
Judith Perani and Norma H. Wolff, *Cloth, Dress and Art Patronage in Africa*
Linda B. Arthur, *Religion, Dress and the Body*
Paul Jobling, Fashion Spreads, *Word and Image in Fashion Photography*
Fadwa El Guindi, *Veil: Modesty, Privacy and Resistance*
Thomas S. Abler, *Hinterland Warriors and Military Dress: European Empires and Exotic Uniforms*
Linda Welters, *Folk Dress in Europe and Anatolia: Beliefs about Protection and Fertility*
Kim K.P. Johnson and Sharron J. Lennon, *Appearance and Power*
Barbara Burman, *The Culture of Sewing*
Annette Lynch, *Dress, Gender and Cultural Change*
Antonia Young, *Women Who Become Men*
David Muggleton, *Inside Subculture: The Postmodern Meaning of Style*
Nicola White, *Reconstructing Italian Fashion: America and the Development of the Italian Fashion Industry*
Brian J. McVeigh, *Wearing Ideology: The Uniformity of Self-Presentation in Japan*
Shaun Cole, *Don We Now Our Gay Apparel: Gay Men's Dress in the Twentieth Century*
Kate Ince, *Orlan: Millennial Female*
Nicola White and Ian Griffiths, *The Fashion Business: Theory, Practice, Image*
Ali Guy, Eileen Green and Maura Banim, *Through the Wardrobe: Women's Relationships with Their Clothes*
Linda B. Arthur, *Undressing Religion: Commitment and Conversion from a Cross-Cultural Perspective*
William J. F. Keenan, *Dressed to Impress: Looking the Part*
Joanne Entwistle and Elizabeth Wilson, *Body Dressing*
Leigh Summers, *Bound to Please: A History of the Victorian Corset*
Paul Hodkinson, *Goth: Identity, Style and Subculture*
Leslie W. Rabine, *The Global Circulation of African Fashion*
Michael Carter, *Fashion Classics from Carlyle to Barthes*
Sandra Niessen, Ann Marie Leshkowich and Carla Jones, *Re-orienting Fashion: The Globalization of Asian Dress*
Kim K.P. Johnson, Susan J. Torntore and Joanne B. Eicher, *Fashion Foundations: Early Writings on Fashion and Dress*
Helen Bradley Foster and Donald Clay Johnson, *Wedding Dress Across Cultures*
Eugenia Paulicelli, *Fashion Under Fascism: Beyond the Black Shirt*
Charlotte Suthrell, *Unzipping Gender: Sex, Cross-Dressing and Culture*
Irene Guenther, *Nazi Chic? Fashioning Women in the Third Reich*
Yuniya Kawamura, *The Japanese Revolution in Paris Fashion*
Patricia Calefato, *The Clothed Body*
Ruth Barcan, *Nudity: A Cultural Anatomy*
Samantha Holland, *Alternative Femininities: Body, Age and Identity*
Alexandra Palmer and Hazel Clark, *Old Clothes, New Looks: Second Hand Fashion*
Yuniya Kawamura, *Fashion-ology: An Introduction to Fashion Studies*
Regina A. Root, *The Latin American Fashion Reader*
Linda Welters and Patricia A. Cunningham, *Twentieth-Century American Fashion*
Jennifer Craik, *Uniforms Exposed: From Conformity to Transgression*
Alison L. Goodrum, *The National Fabric: Fashion, Britishness, Globalization*
Annette Lynch and Mitchell D. Strauss, *Changing Fashion: A Critical Introduction to Trend Analysis and Meaning*
Catherine M. Roach, *Stripping, Sex and Popular Culture*
Marybeth C. Stalp, *Quilting: The Fabric of Everyday Life*
Jonathan S. Marion, *Ballroom: Culture and Costume in Competitive Dance*
Dunja Brill, *Goth Culture: Gender, Sexuality and Style*
Joanne Entwistle, *The Aesthetic Economy of Fashion: Markets and Value in Clothing and Modelling*
Juanjuan Wu, *Chinese Fashion: From Mao to Now*
Brent Luvaas, *DIY Style: Fashion, Music and Global Cultures*
Jianhua Zhao, *The Chinese Fashion Industry*
Eric Silverman, *A Cultural History of Jewish Dress*
Karen Hansen and D. Soyini Madison, *African Dress: Fashion, Agency, Performance*
Maria Mellins, *Vampire Culture*

The Religious Life of Dress

Global Fashion and Faith

Lynne Hume

B L O O M S B U R Y
LONDON • NEW DELHI • NEW YORK • SYDNEY

Bloomsbury Academic

An imprint of Bloomsbury Publishing Plc

50 Bedford Square
London
WC1B 3DP
UK

1385 Broadway
New York
NY 10018
USA

www.bloomsbury.com

Bloomsbury is a registered trade mark of Bloomsbury Publishing Plc

First published 2013

British Library Cataloguing-in-Publication Data
A catalogue record for this book is available from the British Library.

ISBN: HB: 978-08578-5360-8
PB: 978-08578-5361-5
ePDF: 978-1-47256-747-5
ePub: 978-08578-5363-9

Library of Congress Cataloging-in-Publication Data
A catalog record for this book is available from the Library of Congress.

Typeset by Apex CoVantage, LLC, Madison, WI, USA
Printed and bound in Great Britain

Contents

PART II: EASTERN RELIGIONS

PART III: THE MYSTICAL AND THE MAGICAL

Introduction

Religious dress is a visible signifier of difference. The message communicated is that the wearer chooses to follow a certain set of ideological or religious principles and practices. Dress distinctions function to set one religious community apart from other religious communities, and they also operate within a religion to distinguish hierarchies, power structures, gender distinctions, ideas of modesty, roles, mores, group identity and belief and ideology. Religious dress also alters over time, changing according to political pressure from within an institution or group, or outside political and social influences and changes in the prevailing views of morality. Dress can be used to silently express either rebellion or orthodoxy, and when a religion is exported to another culture, some interesting adaptations to an original item of dress might occur. As well, missionaries have been known to enforce punitive measures on indigenes through dress.

The body, writes Joanne Eicher (2010:3), serves as 'an armature, a three-dimensional base for dress'. Dress is defined by Joanne B. Eicher and Mary Ellen Roach-Higgins (1992:15) as: 'an assemblage of modifications of the body and/or supplements to the body'. Throughout this book, I employ the term 'dress' in line with this definition, embracing all material items put *on* the body in the way of clothing, footwear, headgear and other adornments and accoutrements that complete a particular outfit as well as things that are done *to* the body to modify it in some way, such as scarification, tattooing, painting and cosmetics.

Further elaborating on the definition and scope of dress, Eicher, Evenson and Lutz (2008) include the cultural and societal interpretations of what being dressed means as well as how individuals feel about the way they dress. Both these aspects form the paradigm for this book, and the specific aspect of culture that will be discussed is religion.

Religion is a contested concept, one which has no universal definition though many scholars have attempted to provide one. Most agree that religion is an elusive and slippery term that defies the inclusiveness required of a definition that encompasses all beliefs of a religious or spiritual nature. Emile Durkheim's early definition of religion (1915:47) is packed with contentious elements, but it does include 'a unified system of beliefs and practices relative to sacred things' which seems universal and which applies to the major world religions as well as other sacred practices that are less known. Some of these lesser-known sacred practices are included in this volume.

Throughout his many writings, sociologist Max Weber avoided giving a definition of religion; rather, he considered that the task of sociology was to look for the conditions and effects of religion such as (for example) magic and taboo, religious leadership, status groups and so on. Taking this approach, searching for the conditions and effects of religion, dress in all its forms is a reflection of all these things and more. The book is about how religious dress affects the wearers and their relationship to what they believe. Thus, dress itself becomes an active participant in human lives.

The nature of religiosity derives from what Diarmuid Ó Murchú refers to as a 'deep, inner hunger for meaning and connectedness' (2000:192) which takes many and varied forms. As well as the institutionalized religions that have developed doctrine and dogma over hundreds, sometimes thousands of years, more recent forms of religiosity have emerged that reflect more mystical, magical aspects which focus on the experiential. While it is not possible to cover all religious beliefs and practices, those selected for this volume provide a wide sweep of the multitudinous ways in which people are 'religious'.

The way anyone covers, reveals, adds to or in any way decorates his or her body in the name of religious or spiritual beliefs or activities, and the way those beliefs are 'worn', is the book's central focus.

As will be seen, dress does more than merely follow the vagaries of the fashion catwalk, and when it is coupled to religious beliefs, dress itself becomes a sacred item, a statement of ideologies and mores, a contestation of power, a reflection of the spirit world, an active agent in transformation, an access to the supernatural and even a form of punishment. It can be a bridge between the world of the living and the world of the dead. To feel, smell, hear and move with the total ensemble is to give life to religious dress, and in turn, dress can give life to, even transform, its wearer. I therefore emphasize the senses in dress: jewellery that glitters, tinkles, jingles and clangs; fabrics that rustle, shine, cling and change bodily form; the sparkling light from a woman's nose ring; or the constant adjusting and straightening of an unfixed or free-flowing piece of fabric such as a scarf or shawl.

Dress is a communicator of many things (identity, beliefs, the social and political order, individuality, group allegiance) as well as a fashion statement, and placing the totality of dress, and the body in general, within a theoretical framework can be approached in several ways. Mary Douglas (1982) showed how the social body is played out symbolically through the physical body. For

Erving Goffman (1973), dress is one form of nonverbal communication, full of symbolic meanings through which individuals locate themselves within their society, giving them personal and social identity. Pierre Bourdieu (1973) wrote that the body is an unfinished entity that develops according to social forces.

For the most part, dress establishes dichotomies between us and the other, articulating difference from 'them' and sameness with 'us', thus contributing to identity. The control of female sexuality, especially within strictly codified religions, such as some branches of Islam, is played out through its insistence on total coverage of the female body. Bryan Turner (1984:114) highlighted this point when he wrote that 'the sociology of the body is crucially about the control of female sexuality by men exercising patriarchal power'. This is a fine thread running through many religions, as will be seen in the ensuing chapters.

Nathan Joseph (1986:206), taking a neo-Weberian stance, wrote: 'Costumes attempt to express the inexpressible and to rationalize the non-rational. From a social point of view, costume wearers strive to institutionalize and routinize the paradoxical'. Fred Davis (1992:25) suggests that dress is 'a kind of visual metaphor for identity' that involves 'culturally anchored ambivalences'. Jean Comaroff (1985), using her fieldwork among the Tshidi people of South Africa as an example, analysed how the body becomes the mediator between self and society. Equally important is how the dead body is dressed or prepared for the state between life and the afterlife, that liminal period that forms a part of all rites of passage but is most particularly pertinent at death. To discuss all rites of passage is beyond the scope of this book, but I will touch upon how the corpse is clothed according to religious beliefs.

Death is the final rite of passage for us all, and while other rites of passage (birth, puberty, marriage) might be celebrated in most cultures, it is death, when there is a tangible body which has to be handled in some way, that requires the most elaborate treatment with regards to dress and rituals to be performed. At death, beliefs are called into play more than at any other time, and procedures with regard to dress and ceremony are at their most detailed. Does consciousness survive death? Most cultures and religions have their own answers to this question. No matter what one believes, there is still a corpse to be fitted, fashioned and farewelled in an appropriate manner.

A dead body may be mummified, wrapped in a shroud, covered with gold leaf or treated in any one of numerous ways to prepare it for its eventual disintegration and onward journey. The dead body no longer houses the spirit and personality of the person, and yet for a short time, it still resembles that person; it is betwixt and between. It is in a liminal state (Van Gennep 1960) with regard to the world of the living and the world of the spirit, and is sometimes thought to be contaminating to the touch, often viewed with fear and always prepared in a culturally appropriate manner.

In many areas of Melanesia in the South Pacific, parts of the skeleton were kept as relics, particularly the skull of deceased adult men, and carefully preserved as important *sacrae* in cult houses or at sacred sites. Among the Daribi, the corpse's hands, feet or scalp might be cut off as relics, dried over a fire and then pressed beneath a sleeping mat, after which they would be worn around the neck as an expression of sorrow. The Gimi of New Guinea used to practice endocannabilism, the entire body of the deceased being eaten by women. After death and consumption of the corpse, the skull and jaw of a deceased man were commonly worn by the deceased's mother; thereafter, the bones were placed in rock and in tree crevices. Eventually, the spirit was reincarnated as a bird of paradise.

In other parts of the New Guinea Highlands, sorrow at the death of a relative would result in mourners tearing their hair and beards or slicing their earlobes to allow blood to flow; sometimes the tops of fingers were chopped off. By the time they reached adulthood, many Dani women had lost many or most of the finger joints on both hands. Part of the mourning in Melanesia was to restrict bodily adornment for the living, yet the corpse might be dressed fully in his most important ritual finery as a symbol of his status (Knauft 1989:234).

Among the African Yoruba, funeral rites and burials are guided by the circumstances of death. In the case of elders, it is a time for descendants and relatives to come together to celebrate the good life, with the funeral used by the family as an opportunity to display affluence and filial status. It is common for burial to be postponed until funds can be collected for the feasting. Rites are carried out to move the spirit away from the living world and to enable it to be reincarnated. The corpse is traditionally buried under the floor of the house or outside the door in the lineage compound. The often unmarked grave site becomes a focal point where the ancestral spirit can be summoned by pouring libations and calling out praise names of the deceased to encourage the spirit to return to the household of the living when help is needed (Wolff 2004).

It was only with the adoption of Christianity and Islam that designated burial grounds were established among the Yoruba. Bodies of those whose deaths were considered unnatural, such as the corpses of infants and young children, lepers, hunchbacks, albinos, pregnant women, persons killed by lightning or those who hanged themselves, were buried in the bush outside town or in special sacred groves. Suspected witches and wizards might be denied burial, and their bodies would be thrown into bush areas inhabited by wicked spirits (Wolff 2004). In other places in the world, cleaning, bathing, plugging orifices and closing the eyes may be carried out, along with anointing the body with specific substances and adding the culturally prescribed dress.

Often various taboos are associated with the dead, such as not uttering their names, and special behaviour is expected of mourners, especially close relatives. A house in which the deceased died may need to be purified with smoke or even destroyed because of the fear of pollution or that the ghost of the dead may return to cause trouble. All the mirrors in a house might be covered. Widows in many cultures have strict rules to follow, sometimes leading to punitive measures on their own bodies (fingers cut off, hair cut, heavy necklaces worn for many months or mourning clothes worn for long periods) and even death on the funeral pyre of the widow's husband.

How the corpse is disposed of (sky burial, earth burial, second burial, cremation) is culturally explicit and in some instances requires more than one procedure. For example if cremated, the ashes need to be either housed or disposed of, and bones may be kept separately and placed in a reliquary. Some reliquaries, notably those of saints, might have parts of the body, such as finger bones or hair, on display through a transparent 'window' to allow viewers to see inside.

It is clear that dress plays a pivotal part in all aspects of culture; it becomes manifestly important in the realm of religion. This book takes as its theme a culture- and practice-based approach to religious dress, emphasizing the sensorial nature of the subject: the look, smell, feel, touch and even sound of religious apparel; the emotional element of memories and impressions evoked by dress; the textures, materials and kinetic element, from the loose and flowing styles that allow for swaying and twirling, to the strapped, tightened and punitive dress of the more rigid religions or the completely hidden body of total coverage.

Tactile communication between certain people (a man and a menstruating woman; between castes in India) can be considered polluting, necessitating purification rites, while the laying on of hands or the handling of venomous snakes can be proof of belief by the faithful, and the handling of sacred objects such as holy books, or sacred *churinga* (sacred boards in Aboriginal Australia) are acts of devotion and belief. Touch can also convey certain secret knowledge, as in the Masonic handshake, and a kiss can demonstrate love and affection between people, devotion and obeisance (kissing the pope's ring) or respect (the final farewell kiss of the living to the dead). All these tactile demonstrations draw on haptic dynamics and involve the body. Constance Classen (2005, 2012) provides us with fascinating insights into the significance of touch in different cultures and epochs.

Fragrances also can be imbued with moral or religious significance. In Morocco for example foul odours are associated with evil spirits, and a foul-smelling body is vulnerable to evil (Classen, Howes and Synnott 1994); the body needs to pay careful attention to both cleanliness and smell, contributing another aspect to 'dress'. Thieme and Eicher (1990:4) write that dress in Africa 'includes the aspect of gesture, such as when a garment is manipulated when worn' as well as the effects of dress on posture, gait and freedom or restriction of body movement. David Howes refers to the turn toward incorporating all of the senses into academic writing as the 'sensual revolution' and includes the 'sixth sense' (Howes 2009:1).

The Religious Life of Dress reflects the diverse ways people in different religions and spiritualities communicate their inner beliefs through their outward appearance. The book consists of three parts: Part I, Western Monotheistic Religions; Part II, Eastern Religions; and Part III, The Mystical and the Magical. Chapter 1 deals with the way ecclesiastical vestments articulate the powerful male hierarchical structure of the Roman Catholic Church through fabrics, colour and, in some centuries, precious gems, and how the richness of these vestments contrasts with the drab blacks and browns worn by women religious and monastic monks. Changes that were made after Vatican II in the 1960s are also discussed, particularly how they encouraged a more liberal attitude to dress which resulted in some interesting outcomes for women religious. This chapter also follows the results of 'spreading the word' of Christianity via missionaries, as well as some of the dress outcomes due to indigenous influences on Christian vestments.

The pyramid structure of the institution of the Roman Catholic Church reflected in its dress contrasts greatly with the Christian breakaway groups that began to emerge in Europe during the Protestant Reformation of the sixteenth century, exemplified by the Anabaptists' choice of clothing, as will be seen in Chapter 2. Establishing communities in the New World of the Americas, the simple yet highly prescribed practical clothing and lifestyles of the Amish, Hutterites and Mennonites visibly demonstrated the Protestant work ethnic that led them to be dubbed by outsiders as the 'no-frills' people.

Judaism and Islam, the other two major monotheistic religions along with Christianity, are covered in Chapter 3. Viewed through the lens of historical change and denominational differences, we see different degrees of adherence to the interpretive nuances of scriptural passages. Each item of Jewish vesture has religious significance, from the kippa, a small cloth skullcap, to the tallith, a shawl worn during prayer, and the topic of women's head coverings, which can reveal interesting arguments with regard to the percentage of real or synthetic hair permitted in wigs.

Both Jewish and Islamic law requires people to honour their bodies and dress modestly, with both 'honour' and 'modesty' being deciphered according to politics and degree of orthodoxy. Extreme orthodoxy and piety among the Hasidic Jews for example, with their distinguishing black clothing and their long side curls, or *payos*, set them apart from the more liberal branches of Judaism. Total veiling of women in Islam can result in punitive measures for disobedience under rigid political regimes, yet a different interpretation of 'veiling' has resulted in cultural adaptations, demonstrated in the *burqini*, which allows Islamic women to fit in to the Australian beach culture.

Part II, Eastern Religions, focuses on some of the diverse religious beliefs to be found in India (Chapter 4) and Buddhism (Chapter 5). Chapter 4 attempts to convey the sights, sounds and smells of India and the extraordinary colours, textures and styles of this country's many religions. Beginning with Hinduism and its exquisite gold brocades, shimmering silks and mirror-bedecked and sequined fabrics, the ubiquitous sari, with its system of folds and drapes, is described, along with comments on what it feels like to wear a sari. I then move to *sadhus*, India's itinerant holy people, and their individual ways of displaying their vows of renunciation from the world, followed by the perfectly groomed monotheistic Sikhs, whose turbans and symbols display their commitment to cleanliness, truth and fighting for what is right, in the five symbols worn on their bodies, known as the five 'Ks'. Finally, this chapter examines the Jains, whose quintessence is nonviolence which extends to nonviolent means of cloth production.

Chapter 5 then moves to Buddhism, investigating the importance of the robe to Buddhist philosophy and practices. It will be seen that from its earliest beginnings to the present the robe is an intrinsic part of a religion based on kindness and compassion and the high spiritual ideals of following the Buddha, mastering the Dharma and being a part of the Sangha, the religious community. 'Taking the robe', an item of dress that dates back 2,500 years, is the ultimate expression of monastic commitment to the teachings of the Buddha.

In Part III, there is a change of direction away from the major world religions to the mystical and magical, which are represented in this part by three distinctly different groups: the Sufis, shamans and modern pagans, different in many ways but alike in their mystical/magical approach to spirituality and technologies for accessing the 'divine' or altering consciousness. Chapter 6 begins with the rapture of the Sufis and their deep love of God, danced out in their mystical whirling movements, their wide bell-like skirted frocks forming a triangular pattern. I then move to the shamans' apparel and paraphernalia which help them to access, through trance techniques, other realities or other worlds. Finally, the dress of modern pagans is discussed, dress that displays and aids their 'magical selves' to take flight into realms of magic and ritual. The dress of both shamans and pagans can vary greatly from very simple to highly elaborate or from nude to fantastic and ornate.

Religions of possession are perused in Chapter 7 with Vodou, Candomblé and Santería, three religions that stem originally from Africa. In these highly charged, exciting and colourful ceremonies, participants call on the spirits to enter their physical bodies. Once possessed of a particular spirit they are then clothed accordingly, perhaps in a black top hat, striped pants and a skeleton-like appearance if Baron Samdi appears or in snake vertebrae when Dambala, the spirit associated with snakes, makes his appearance. We read what it feels like to be possessed, and the sounds and smells of the clothes moving with the will of the spirit inhabiting the possessed person's body to the accompaniment of frenzied drumming and chanting.

There are of course many other religions and spiritualities that are not covered in this book, but the above have been chosen to articulate the enormous spread of beliefs, ideas and associated religious dress to be found throughout the world. As well, within most religions there are notable variations between levels of orthodoxy and liberalism. The focus here will be on the more orthodox groups as they quite often visibly demonstrate their adherence to orthodoxy as a means of separating themselves from the more liberal groups within a religion and from the world outside their religion. In many cases dress becomes 'fossilized fashion' (Gordon 1987; Arthur 1998) where an original dress item or ensemble from times past is maintained into the present with little or no variation in presentation, emphasizing even more the wearer's dress as a boundary marker of separateness.

Throughout the book I touch upon the way religions might call upon the modification and enhancement of the body itself, in addition to the garb that is put on the body. The skin is the outer surface, the protective veil between inside and outside, providing a canvas upon which to illustrate belief. It can be tattooed, scarified, painted, pierced and branded to communicate identity and ideology.

Noninvasive and temporary decorative practices use ochre, paint and dyes such as henna, which are all easily removed. More invasive and permanent body markings are made through tattooing and scarification and are often used to permanently mark an important event in a person's life. Tattooing has a long history and can articulate inclusion or exclusion of the tattooed person within a particular community. Another form of body modification is piercing, exemplified by the two-day Hindu festival called Thaipusam, where men, women and boys practice self-mortification through carrying the *kavadi*, which pierces the flesh.

In sum, using a sensorial approach to dress as it is applied to religion, this volume offers an overview of beliefs and spiritual practices globally expressed through the specifics of fabric, ensembles and accoutrements; the feel of an entire outfit, the way it moves with the body, the emotions associated with it, the memories evoked, the smells and the transformative process that occurs when one dons sacred garments. Dress is more than a visual demonstration of allegiance to a particular set of beliefs. It is a sensory testimony of those beliefs.

PART I

WESTERN MONOTHEIST RELIGIONS

−1−

Hierarchies and Power: Christianity and the Roman Catholic Church

Most religions begin with one person and a simple message. However, when the leader dies and the religion is sustained despite the leader's death, it may spread far and wide, and the number of followers may burgeon into hundreds, thousands and even millions. When this occurs, a hierarchy inevitably develops, and a powerful political system arises, with the differentials of power and authority displayed through dress.

Throughout the history of Christianity, dress has also been employed as a moral discursive about shame, modesty and sexuality. The earliest Christian moralists looked to the Old Testament, especially Isaiah, for Biblical confirmation of their disdain for the excesses of shameful and immodest dress. Passages in Isaiah 3:16 and 3:24 (cited in Ribeiro 2003 [1986]:19) reveal sentiments on the disagreeable sensual nature of some dress, referring to movement, sound, smell and the visual properties of apparel:

> daughters of Zion . . . [who] walk with stretched forth necks and wanton eyes, walking and mincing as they go, and making a tinkling with their feet . . . the Lord will take away the bravery of their tinkling ornaments about their feet . . . all their other jewellery and the changeable suits of apparel . . . And it shall come to pass, that instead of sweet smell there shall be stink; instead of a girdle a rent; and instead of well-set hair baldness; and instead of a stomacher a girding of sackcloth; and burning instead of beauty.

Other passages in Isaiah denounced the 'showy adornments' and 'allurements of beauty' as being only for the likes of prostitutes and 'shameless women'. One of the early Christian Church fathers, Tertullian, is quoted as saying: 'Woman, you are the gateway of the devil. You persuaded him whom the devil dared not attack directly. Because of you the son of God had to die. You should always go dressed in mourning and in rags.'

Men were not omitted from scriptural moral denouncements. In 1 Corinthians 2:14 for example men were urged never to shave their beards, as beards distinguished the Christian from the clean-shaven pagan Roman, and as for hair on the head, God had counted every hair, and it must remain intact. Fine and fancy clothes were thought to contrast adversely to the simple attire of the truly spiritual man whose clothing merely demonstrated the practical functions of warmth and bodily coverage.

In the early years before Christianity became a full-fledged religion, it was expected that followers of Christ would wear clothing for decency and warmth rather than for show. There was even a deliberate rejection of special garments for the emerging clergy (Ribeiro 2003 [1986]). Apart from the various kinds of circular hooded mantles which were part of 'barbarian' wear, ecclesiastical vestments arose mainly out of Roman secular dress. Some of the garments still worn today, such as the alb, were traditionally made of linen, wool or a cotton blend and can be traced directly to the ancient Roman clothing worn by Roman citizens in the early days of Christianity.

The hierarchical nature of the Roman Catholic Church[1] today is reflected in its ecclesiastical vestments, from the pope who presides at the top of a pyramid structure through various levels to the local parish priest.

Throughout its history, there has been an overt display of rich vestments: expensive fabrics such as silk, furs such as ermine and, in some centuries, precious gems, all in stark contrast to Christianity's humble beginnings.

Figure 1.1 Pope Benedict XVI, Italy, 2012. Photo: Getty Images.

Such wealth of garments, however, has graced the male body uniquely, articulating not only rank but also male focus and power. Each rank is made stunningly apparent by the use of specific colours for vestments, with scarlets and purples contrasting with the unique white. Overall, one's rank is shown as black for seminarians, deacons, priests and chaplains; violet for bishops, prelates and protonotaries; scarlet for cardinals; and white for the supreme representative and head of the Roman Catholic Church, the pope. Hierarchical colours are strikingly evident when one of the layers of this system congregates together. A large group of cardinals for example makes a splendid splash of colour in their red and white vestments.

In contrast, the female dress of the Roman Catholic Church lacks the elaborate richness of the male hierarchy and is much more modest. It is devoid of colour, being usually black or black and white, articulating the lowly status of women religious compared to the men and their deep commitment to holy and modest clothing.

This has not been consistently the case however. In the early eighth century, when there was relatively little difference between the dress of the clergy and that of the laity, many of the female religious orders were composed of women from 'ladies of rank', used to dressing for life in the world rather than for life in cloistered confines, a world that would have included

Figure 1.2 Two Roman Catholic nuns, Germany. Photo: Getty Images.

the wearing of fine clothes. Such finery was a subject of great concern to St Aaldhelm, who wrote in the eighth century:

> Silk underclothing . . . scarlet tunics and hoods, sleeves with silk stripes, shoes edged with fur; hair carefully arranged on forehead and temples with the curling iron—this is the modern habit. Dark veils yield to headdresses white and coloured, sewn with long ribbons and hanging to the ground; fingernails are sharpened like the talons of hawks or owls seeking their prey. (quoted in Ribeiro 2003 [1986]:32)

Such luxury was viewed as excessive and 'hateful to God'. Particular condemnation was given to dresses whose colours were scarlet or purple, as these colours were considered to lead to 'lust, unholy intercourse, indifference to reading and prayer, and the ruin of souls', a curious statement in view of the purple and red that are worn now by those in the upper echelons of the Church. Choices of colours, fabrics and other decorations considered suitable for wear by the holy have fluctuated over the centuries to a marked degree.

The central vestment of the Roman Catholic Church is the *cassock*, which has not changed since the twelfth century (another example of 'fossilized fashion' mentioned in the Introduction), when it was dropped by the laity and adapted for ecclesiastical wear. The cassock, topped with a Roman collar, is a floor-length item with thirty-three buttons in total, representing Christ's earthly years. The cassock colours follow the ranking system mentioned above.[2] The *simar* (or *zimarra*) resembles the cassock and has an additional shoulder cape of the same fabric and colour. It is always black (except for the pope's *simar,* which is white). It is trimmed in scarlet for cardinals and red for bishops. The *simar* evolved from the cassock and became a unique vestment in the late eighteenth century. The *fascia* is the sash around the waist which functions as a belt. Again, colours are white for the pope, scarlet for a cardinal, violet for a bishop and black for others.

The *chasuble* is the major liturgical vestment of a priest or a bishop and resembles a long, sleeveless poncho-like cloak. It matches the liturgical colours and is worn over the alb (a long white vestment, tied at the waist with a cincture). The chasuble developed from the worker's practical cloak (*casula*) as protection in the fields during inclement weather. By the third century, the cloak was worn by all Christians, and later, in the time of Emperor Alexander Severus, it became restricted to the clergy.

The hierarchical nature of the institution of the Roman Catholic Church is also reflected in its headdresses. The *zucchetto*, a silk skullcap, originated in the very early Church as the covering of the clerical tonsure (shaved crown of the head), and during the Middle Ages and early Renaissance, different colours were allowed to indicate the hierarchical ranks: white for the pope, scarlet for a cardinal and violet for a bishop; priests may use a black cloth zucchetto for everyday wear but not during the liturgy. In the Middle Ages, priests were usually not wealthy men, and most wore simple woollen robes except during church services when they wore many layers of beautiful vestments: albs (long belted tunics of white linen), dalmatics (long unbelted surcoats worn on top of albs), chasubles and ornate capes.

Bishops wore the same type of garments as priests celebrating Mass, but they also wore large triangular hats, called *mitres*, to indicate their importance, and they carried crosiers, tall, hooked walking sticks that symbolized the simple shepherd's walking stick, a relic of humility.

Palliums, circular bands of white lamb's wool decorated with five red or black crosses, and long streamers covered an archbishop's shoulders, and he carried tall crosses covered in jewels. A medieval pope dressed mostly in a white linen robe, a red or white cloak called a papal mantle, red stockings, red shoes and a red cape when outside. A small red cap was also worn under his mitre, and during processions and ceremonies, he wore a crown (Steele 2005).

Figure 1.3 Roman Catholic bishops from around the world at St Peter's Square, Vatican City, 2012. Photo: Getty Images.

In its simplest form, the mitre, a tall headdress worn at liturgical functions, is made of layered white damask silk or white linen without any embellishments. The origins of the mitre date back to pre-Christian Greece, when it was worn by Greek athletes. The ribbons attached to the mitre predate the hat itself and were attached to a laurel wreath that circled the head of the winner of an athletic competition. The pontifical mitre is said to be of Roman origin. When the early Christian hierarchy adopted it as papal vesture, the hat became taller and more ornamental.

At the height of the Church's power around the year 1054, when the Roman Catholic Church split from the Orthodox Church of the Byzantine Empire, the pope in Rome was viewed by the people as God's representative on earth and dressed in splendid robes and jewels, wearing a type of crown as a symbol of his power, articulating his equal status with royalty. A papal tiara had been worn by all popes from the ninth century, and by the time of Pope Benedict XII, who died in 1342, the tiara was ringed by three crowns arranged in tiers. From a small crown with points at the side, by the end of the twelfth century, the mitre had developed into a large, cloth-covered cylinder, embroidered and beribboned, split into points at the front and back.

Many mitres in the Middle Ages were decorated with very costly ornamentation: rich embroidery, pearls, and precious stones and metals. In the seventeenth and eighteenth centuries, it became even more imposing, when, along with as many as several hundred precious stones and pearls, heavy gold embroidery was added, making it an uncomfortably heavy item of clothing to wear on the head and no doubt resulting in headaches for the wearer. From the early simple white linen mitre, it developed into an item that was the symbol of a grand and imposing display of wealth.

The pope continues to wear a mitre, and cardinals wear mitres in the presence of the pope. Around the eleventh century, bishops were allowed to wear them. Unlike other vestments, the mitre is removed when the wearer prays, reflecting the Apostolic commandment that a man should pray with the head uncovered.

The *biretta*, a square-shaped hat with silk trim and tuft and three raised wings (curiously called 'horns'), evolved from the soft square academic hat of the high Middle Ages (specifically from Milan, Italy). The biretta is the ancestor of the modern academic mortarboard (which is still worn by students and faculty at most university graduation ceremonies). A biretta is scarlet for cardinals, violet for bishops and black for priests, deacons and seminarians.

Adornments include the *pectoral cross* and rings. The pectoral cross, developed as a reliquary of the True Cross on which Christ was crucified, is a small cross, suspended by a cord or chain and worn around the neck close to the heart. The pope's ring, known as the fisherman's ring, is a very personal item, as it bears the unique seal of the reigning pontiff and is destroyed at his death. Cardinals wear the cardinalatial ring, and bishops wear the episcopal ring. Ancient in origin, the ring first appeared as an episcopal symbol in the third century. By the seventh century, each new bishop was given a ring as a gift from the pope.

The open and public display of earthly riches and lavish dress of the Church became a point of contention among some Christian groups, the latter objecting to the stark contrast between what the Church had become, with its power and authority reflected in the sumptuous reds, velvets and rich brocades, and the simple message of Christ.

From the tenth century onwards, some preferred to live their lives in spiritual communities, monasteries and convents, forming different 'orders' of monks and nuns who wished to devote themselves to a communal religious life of humility and poverty, favouring simple clothing along with a simple lifestyle, devoting themselves to prayer, to study and to caring for people in need. Their tunics and habits were often made of rough, itchy wool, dyed black, grey or white, over which they wore scapulars, robes open at the sides. Monks sometimes wore cowls, or hoods, and shaved the top and base of their heads, leaving a thin band of hair around the scalp, called a tonsure.

WOMEN RELIGIOUS

Women religious, or nuns, wore simple habits with a wimple, a cloth covering their head and neck. Both the Dominicans and the Franciscans took vows of poverty; the former chose to wear white gowns and black caps, the latter a hooded, or cowled, brown habit, girdled with rope and knotted to remind them of their vows. The Carmelites chose white and brown stripes for their habits, and the Carthusians chose plain white. Coexisting with Christian beliefs and practices were the old pagan beliefs and religious festivals, with participants adorning themselves with masks, clothes, leaves and flowers, banging drums and mocking the upper classes and the Church by sometimes dressing a goat as a bishop to preside over 'misrule' (Steele 2005:23). Some of these practices have continued to the present, and others have been revived or reinvented by modern-day pagans.

By the twelfth and thirteenth centuries in Europe, chastity and virginity were expected of women and became highly desirable qualities. The chaste and enclosed woman was personified in the figure of the nun, set apart in her community of virginal women, each one sleeping alone in a small, sparse cell, with only thoughts of her bridegroom, Christ. Anchorite communities consisted of nuns separated from the world who took vows of stability, obedience and chastity. Many of these women came from the English and Anglo-Norman upper classes. The early thirteenth-century *Guide for Anchoresses* encouraged women to control any temptations, to confess any wrong deed or thought and to do penance for any sins that might escape their control. Penitential zealots went to extreme lengths in their passionate moments of devotion to Christ, wanting to experience the suffering of Christ on the cross.

In the thirteenth and fourteenth centuries, the focus on a suffering Christ increased and immeasurable love was married to immeasurable pain. The Bride of Christ wanted to suffer the agonies of her 'husband'. The self-punitive measures of ascetics included extreme forms of fasting, with some living only on the sacraments, and wearing metal chains fastened around the waist so tightly that they pinched and tore the skin. Some bound their arms and bodies tightly with rough and itchy horsehair garments, called *cilicia*, or vines of thorns, or regularly engaged in self-flagellation using ropes or metal chains; others perforated their feet with nails or knelt on iron spikes (Flynn 1996:258). Such torturous treatment of the body resulted in catatonic seizures, bodily rigidity and, on rare occasions, stigmatic wounds. All these bleak practices were not without spiritual results however, and penitents reported divine encounters, revelations, visions and a 'fusion with the crucified body of Christ' (Bynum 1987:208–9).

The severity and frequency of such actions prompted warnings and prohibitions from concerned Church quarters, and rules about such extreme behaviour led to statements such as the following:

> Nobody should . . . wear anything made of iron or hair or hedgehog skins, or beat herself with them, or with a scourge weighted with lead, with holly, or with thorns, or draw blood, without her confessor's permission. She should not sting herself anywhere with nettles, or scourge the front of her body, or mutilate herself with cuts, or take excessively severe disciplines at any one time, in order to subdue temptations. (cited in Wogan-Browne 1994:33)

During these times some pious men experienced visions and other experiences of God, but women ascetics tended towards the sensual and erotic, to the extent that the German mystic David of Augsburg (d. 1271) openly ridiculed them as 'erotic ticklings' and was 'a bit suspicious of such piety' (Bynum 1991:169). The Roman Catholic saint Ignatius of Loyola (b. 1491) cautioned that although penance through pain should be felt by the flesh, it should not penetrate to the bones (Longridge 1919:74).

The dress of nuns, universally known as the 'habit', was homogeneous; the intention, like all dress of a uniform nature, was to focus on the community's ideals and beliefs, rather than on those of the individual. The term 'habit' refers to the ensemble of clothing and accessories that make up the complete dress of women religious in the Roman Catholic Church. It conceals the body and absorbs the self into a collective whole, thus effectively suppressing individuality and articulating a distinct detachment from earthly matters. By adopting the habit, women religious publicly became part of a new spiritual family; the body, dress and daily life were set according to religious conventions and rules and complete obedience was expected. Once secular clothes were replaced by the black religious garb of the nun, they were clothed in sanctity and promised body and soul to their order. In most orders,

> The uniform was characterized by complete simplicity and modesty, being high-necked, long-sleeved and ankle length. In addition to the uniform, feminine lingerie was exchanged for simple white cotton underwear, indicating that the postulant was exchanging her womanly enjoyments for austere dress that would now symbolize her as the spouse of Jesus Christ. In addition, henceforth the woman was no longer to be distinguished by dress from the other women in the institute with whom she would live. (Ebaugh 1977:21–2)

The origin of the habit was the widow's dress of the day. The Sisters of St Joseph began in France in the seventeenth century with just six widows who began to minister to the needs of people. Any hint of fleshly sensuality was secreted under voluminous dresses of black serge and veils that covered their bodies from head to toe. Visibly identified as widows, they were able to move around more freely than married women and the taint of widowhood allowed them to travel unhindered without male chaperones (Michelman 1999; Aherne 1983).

The habit consists basically of the plain wide-sleeved tunic, veil, belt, scapular, cloak and simple footwear, which has varied little throughout the centuries. The tunic's T-shape was reminiscent of the Cross of Calvary; to wear it was to clothe oneself in the mystery of the Passion. The 'veil' is the long cloth worn on the top of the head, extending down the back. It is usually attached to a cap underneath, or 'coif', which is a close-fitting cloth headpiece that conforms to the shape of the skull. A 'wimple', or 'guimpe', is the fabric piece that covers the neck and chest and sometimes extends over the chin. A 'bandeau' is the piece that stretches across the forehead, often attached at the ears behind the veil. A 'scapular' is a long apron-like garment worn over the tunic that extends down both the front and the back of the tunic to floor length. A 'cincture' is a belt worn around the waist of the tunic, and a 'rosary' is a string of prayer beads and other objects often attached to the cincture and worn at the side. A *cappa* (cape) refers to the cloak that is worn over the tunic (Kuhns 2003).

Clothed in stark black and white habits, with starched white linen head-bands and wimples and long heavy woolen dresses with flowing black veils, the nuns were noticeably set apart from their secular sisters throughout the centuries, giving them an air of separateness and holiness. What demarcated specific orders of nuns throughout the centuries was principally the distinctive headgear of each order (Hume 2010).

Because Christianity was not the official religion of the Roman Empire until late in the fourth century, it is unlikely that the nun's habit originated in its earliest years as an imposition by the Church. Initially, the nun's habit was simply a voluntary choice by its wearer to mark the woman's desired path to saintliness. Lowly and simple clothing was meant to contrast with the clothing of the privileged classes. Some of the higher classes even donned their own servants' garments as a demonstration of faith. Women religious date to the very inception of the church, however, and the earliest images of nuns are found in missals and other liturgical books (Sisters of Mercy, Brisbane 2004).

A veil consecration rite was in effect as early as the second century. The earliest Christians who wished to consecrate their lives to God sometimes donned sacred garb without ceremony or clerical oversight, privately transforming their outward appearance to reflect their spiritual commitment. By the middle of the tenth century, the clothing ceremony for many nuns represented an elaborate secular marriage ceremony. The novitiate was given away by her father or male guardian at which time she became the Bride of Christ, espoused to the Heavenly Bridegroom.

Many regulations regarding modesty and the absence of vanity related directly to the body. A nun not only was modestly dressed but also was advised to keep 'custody of the eyes', being careful not to look a man directly in the eye and to keep the gaze away from worldly places such as shop windows; mirrors were considered a sign of vanity. She was directed to keep her voice low and to walk in a calm, demure manner, with the hands out of sight underneath the scapular, and as close to the walls as she could. Because of the physically rigid restrictions of the headbands worn by the nuns, many developed deep ridges over their eyebrows where the headband rested for many years or developed migraine headaches from headgear that was too tight (Michelman 1999; McLay 1996; Sisters of Mercy, Brisbane 2004).

There were carefully prescribed guidelines for the order in which the nuns dressed, and each piece of clothing had to be kissed and a prayer recited while donning it. The long dress, loosely tied at the waist with a cincture, demonstrated her renouncement of worldliness and the insignificance of the body. The dress was loosely tied to symbolize chastity as the wearer recited a prayer to request that she be girded with purity and that the passion of lust be removed from her veins. Then the coif, or hair- and face-enclosing headpiece, was put on to signify innocence and simplicity. A veil symbolizing virginity was pinned onto the coif. Finally, the scapular, or tunic, bearing the insignia of the convent, was placed over the dress (McLay 1996).

VATICAN II AND CHANGES

From the 1950s onwards, there was an escalating move away from biblical literalism and towards integrating modern human experience with Church dogma, the aim being to initiate a dialogue with the contemporary world. The Second Ecumenical Council of the Vatican, more commonly referred to as Vatican II, opened under Pope John XXIII in 1962 and closed under Pope Paul VI in 1965. It affected virtually all aspects of Catholic life. The main goals of the council were to bring the Church in line with the modern world, to attempt to create a new vision of ecumenism and to reinterpret the liturgy so as to encourage participation of all members of the Catholic Church.

Among the sweeping reforms that ensued from Vatican II were those that pertained to ecclesiastical dress. The religious dress reforms created a 'seismic shift' (Keenan 2000:86), collapsing centuries of uniformity and Church restrictions on the body. They were to influence Roman Catholic dress around the world and result, in some instances, in more changes than could be anticipated. Two monastic orders, the Marist Brothers and the Sisters of Mercy, are examples of those changes.

Vatican II and the Marist Brothers

The Marist Brothers order was founded in 1817 by Father Marcellin Champagnat (1789–1840), a village priest trained in Lyon, France. During his seminary years, he was an active founding member of the Society of Mary, and his small band of followers became known as the 'Little Brothers of Mary', a group of enthusiastic devotees who viewed Mary as their Divine Mother and protectress. They dressed uniformly and simply, in a blue coat that reached just below the knee, black trousers, a small cloak and a round hat, referred to as the 'Livery of Mary'. Their early enthusiasm was later to be subsumed by the Church's regulations and its propensity for reason and rationality (Keenan 2000).

After Champagnat's death in 1840, the Little Brothers eventually became a fully fledged religious order within the Church; the Marist Brothers and their clothing became more regulated and controlled, with every detail codified according to Church stipulations. There were significant changes to the early Marist Brothers' dress, and, like all other religious communities, instructions from the Vatican ensured that religious dress adhered to minutely detailed dress regulations. From 1863 to 1962, an epoch that has been referred to as the 'Uniform Century', Vatican authorities stipulated that clothing had to be 'plain, modest, and conformable to evangelical poverty' and that the Brothers were to wear

a triangular hat, a white rabat, a soutane of black cloth, closing in front with hooks and eyes in the middle, then sewn to the bottom (of the soutane); a mantle of the same cloth as the soutane, and long enough to cover the arms stretched out; cloth or linen stockings, not knitted but sewn; shoes with laces; those who have made the Vow of Obedience shall wear, besides, a woollen cord, and the Professed Brothers a cross. (Keenan 2000:91)

Gone were the days of the simple community of Marist Brothers, dressed in the loosely prescribed outfits established by Champagnat, to be replaced by strict uniformity in both the quality of material and the manner of wearing such dress. Keenan (2000:92) writes:

The dress tradition of the Brothers had become sclerotic, frozen in the icy grip of bureaucratic regulation, the spiritual eloquence of its unique 'Marian' voice rendered silent.

This standardization of dress followed the Marist Brothers from Europe to Latin America, North America, Asia, Africa and Australia. The Marist Directory set out minute details of every item of apparel, from the length of the hem of the soutane and the fastening of their cloaks, to how they might carry their cloaks when not worn ('suspended from their arm' and 'with the collar turned towards their body'). Other requirements included sewn (not knitted) stockings, cotton pocket handkerchiefs and shoes of cowhide leather covering the whole foot, fastened with mohair or cotton shoelaces. They were to have their hair cut every two months, each man with exactly the same cut. No gloves were to be worn, and they were to use a standard religious umbrella that was the same as all others. Even the quantity of each item of apparel was the same for each of the brothers (Keenan 2000).

The Marist dress code thus became fixed until Vatican II relaxed these rigid dress stipulations in 1962. By the 1990s, we see the Marist Brothers dressed in clothes that are indistinguishable from the nonclerical male population, albeit showing a decidedly conservative style: open shirts, relaxed trousers, simple cardigans or sweaters and their own choice of shoes. Church expectations were only that the brothers wear clothing characterized by simplicity and modesty, avoiding worldly vanity. Alternatively, they could wear a Roman collar, or rabat, a cord or, for those permanently professed, a crucifix.

Women Religious and Change

The twentieth century was also a time of great change in the clothing of women religious. While the habit was recognized and respected by more people than in any previous century, it began to be seen as antiquated clothing, symbolizing remoteness from the outside society that they were striving to serve. The 1950s particularly was a decade of radical transformation in the lives of many nuns all over the world. Between 1950 and 1960, there was a huge demand for their teaching and nursing services, and they became visibly of, and in, the world rather than hidden away in cloisters. The women looked at the unsuitability of their clothing for practical work in the modern world (McLay 1996; Michelman 1999; Sisters of Mercy, Brisbane 2004).

Clothing restrictions were relaxed after the Second Ecumenical Council of the Vatican in 1962, and nuns exchanged habits for clothing that was less restrictive; however, it was not always an easy transition. Many experienced the use of their peripheral vision for the first time since their youth. Once headdresses were removed or replaced there were some unfortunate side effects: a common problem was that their hair was in terrible condition—often thin and patchy—from constantly being under wraps, years of poor circulation, and friction beneath layers of fabric. For some, body weight became an issue once the flowing habit was discarded for more form-fitting modern clothes (McLay 1996; Michelman 1999).

Women who had never worn make-up or jewellery began to look around for advice on these aspects of their persona. For some, it was a liberating experience; for others, it was confusing and troublesome. Elderly nuns espe-cially suffered from these new introductions to clothing; some did not want to discard the habit as it was the ultimate symbol of their lives. For these women, it was an emotionally draining process. The changes were very painful, not only for the nuns themselves but also for laywomen who were used to seeing the nuns as some sort of icon, an extension of their own identity as Catholic women, a revered extension that set women religious apart from themselves.[3]

Values also changed along with the garb. Many women left religious life altogether and ventured out into the world; there was a dramatic decline in the numbers of women religious. Once the 'squeezing of the transcen-dent' (Berger 1970) was allowed to be reversed, some of them wished to find new rituals and symbols that better expressed their theology and spirituality. The 1960s and onward was a time of great upheaval in the secular world of women as well, when the first consciousness-raising groups began to discuss women's issues, women and society, and women and religion. Women were allowed into theological colleges for the first time and started to question the male emphasis of the scriptural translations, as well as the position of women in the Church.[4]

Both secular and nonsecular women started to look around for new directions in their spiritual lives and began to converse with one another. The Sisters of Mercy are a good example of this shift.

Vatican II and the Sisters of Mercy

Stemming from the upheaval brought about by many social changes in the twentieth century, the Second Vatican Council's decisions and the issues with regard to the position and rights of women, both inside and outside the Church, many women began to question their own lives. Some of the Mercy Sisters reflected on the reasons that they had entered the Church when they were young women and discovered that Church dogma and the patriarchal nature of the Church had somehow taken them far from the spiritual nature of their vocations.[5]

Some explored their own cultural backgrounds and engaged in much soul-searching, delving into their unconscious beliefs, attitudes and longings through a series of meditative processes, arriving at some significant issues of concern. The background to the Sisters of Mercy was relevant to this soul-searching as it affected their changes in attitudes.

The order of the Sisters of Mercy was founded in Ireland in the early nine-teenth century, and from that location their communities spread to other parts of the world, including one that has operated out of southern Queensland, Australia, since 1861. As women with a predominantly Irish background, when they began to question their spirituality, they discussed how they felt about their 'place' in the world. The Australian Sisters of Mercy found that some of their dissatisfaction was related to a loss of place, or rootedness, and feelings of disconnection to homeland. They pondered what all these factors might actually mean to them and to their religious beliefs.

Some explored indigenous Australian spirituality. Some wished to find new rituals and symbols that better expressed their theology and spirituality, and several returned to Ireland for short sojourns to find their own sense of deep connection. While still retaining their faith as Roman Catholics, they also found that Celtic symbols and lore held significance for them in order to combine their past, present and future. The *triskele*, a Celtic symbol that consists of triple concentric spirals engraved on ancient Celtic monuments, was adopted as their logo for what it was that they wanted to express about themselves, and some began incorporating this and other Celtic symbols into their dress.[6]

Looking at the significance of 'place' to other cultures within Australia led to conversations with Aboriginal women, as well as non-Christian women who followed both Goddess spirituality and nature religion. Dialogues ensued between all these women's groups, and in various workshops, they all expressed their differences and similarities. The nuns incorporated ritual, symbol and storytelling in their discussions and exchanged and shared different viewpoints, understandings and insights, all in light of their Catholic tradition. During that exploration and searching, the Celtic symbols and reflection on a Celtic hereditary past took them into the uncharted waters of paganism, pagan rites and the sacredness of religious sites that were not confined to church buildings.

This affected their dress at a subtle level and became outwardly apparent in the employment and use of symbols, colour, and jewellery and the way they set up their altars with goddess and nature symbols that were more reflective of the changes they discovered in themselves. The stark black-and-white habit disappeared to be replaced by clothing that was modern and colourful, with jewellery that incorporated some Celtic symbols and Goddess features. The change in viewpoints of this community of sisters was historically mirrored through their change in dress.

In less than forty years, they moved from full habit to modified habit with shorter dress lengths and short veils, to clothes that did not distinguish them from any other Australian woman. Each woman selected her own dress style, some choosing to wear jewellery that indicated their interest in women's spirituality, Celtic Goddess figures and ancient spiral symbols. Their separateness was no longer visible, thus dissolving many of the communication barriers that their religious habits had established, allowing them more freedom and accessibility with other women. They still identified as Roman Catholic sisters, but they viewed themselves as having moved in a spiral that had taken them on a spiritual journey to the heart of why they had become nuns in the first place.

Other Christian Denominations

Apart from the Roman Catholics and the monastic orders, there are numerous other Christian denominations, which fall along a continuum with regard to dress, from the highly elaborate at one end to extreme simplicity at the other end. A less extensive hierarchical display of dress is seen in some Protestant denominations (such as Anglicans), while in the evangelical stream of Christianity, the dress of ministerial leaders does not differ from that of their congregations. When Christianity spread to other cultures, dress changed yet again.

SPREADING THE WORD: MISSIONS, AUTHORITY AND THE INDIGENIZATION OF CHRISTIANITY

Protestant and Catholic Missions

Missionaries invariably sought to stamp out indigenous practices which they felt were in opposition to the moral order. The shift from polytheism, in those regions where it was practiced, to monotheism began in the late 1890s as a result of missionary influence.

While missionary zeal, for the most part, had good intentions, the main goal being to care for and protect native people, there has been a mixed result, with some cultures being severely crippled as a result of contact with both Westerners as a whole and Western missionaries as agents of dramatic change (see Swain and Rose 1988; Hume 1988). Christian missionaries of all denominations were very active in spreading their message throughout the world, and as a result of Christian ideas about morality, there were a variety of dress modifications and adaptations in the regions and cultures in which missionaries lived. Missionaries of many Christian denominations introduced modest attire among the communities to which they were sent, usually far-flung outposts thousands of miles from their European homelands.

During the nineteenth and early twentieth centuries, missionary zeal was at its pinnacle, and invariably one of the main aims, along with conversion, was to cover the naked or scantily clad body of the 'heathens'. Conversion and European dress went hand in hand, as the older style dress used in traditional religious practices was rejected by missionaries as a relic of pre-Christian pagan practices. Introduced European dress, along with the fabrics used by European dressmakers and tailors, mimicked the clothing worn by Europeans. Many formal photographs from those decades show unsmiling, puzzled indigenes in the same style of dress as that worn by their masters and missionaries.

The next section will look firstly at some of the dress changes that occurred because of missionary influence, and then at how indigenous people themselves brought their own influence on dress once they chose to become Christian priests, ministers or women religious, resulting in innovative combinations of dress.

Dress Changes due to Missionary/European Influence

Christianity, in its visible form, adapts and adopts culturally when it is exported. 'Mother Hubbard' dresses that cover some South Pacific indigenous women's bodies are only one example that indicate the moral attributes of the clothed body in contrast to the 'uncivilized' and 'immoral' unclothed or barely clothed body of the indigenes.

The Mother Hubbard dress, also referred to as 'grandmother's dress', introduced by missionaries and worn as early as the 1880s in various Polynesian islands,[7] is still worn today in Tahiti and New Caledonia. A Mother Hubbard dress is a long, wide, loose-fitting gown with long sleeves and a high neck, often made in bright floral cotton, usually with large hibiscus flowers as a print. In New Caledonia in the South Pacific, one of the popular tourist attractions is to watch New Caledonian women playing their own special style of cricket wearing these dresses, called in French *robes missions* (mission dresses).[8]

In Africa, the Americas, Australia and the Pacific Islands, dress adaptations reflect the specific cultures of the inhabitants and these are sometimes woven into liturgical vestments. Aboriginal Australians for example have designed their own copes with Aboriginal motifs; Roman Catholic saints have been incorporated into Vodou in the Americas, forming part of the rich fabric of this religion; and Yoruba have re-introduced traditional aspects into religious dress.

Yoruba, Africa

Traditional Yoruba[9] religious ritual practices included worship of various nature deities and other deities known generally as *orisha*. The followers of some of these deities wore locally handwoven cloths, made with handspun cotton thread when participating in particular rituals. One such ritual called for white cloth (*aso ala*) that was tied with a red cloth. Some also attached cowrie shells to 'big' red skirts or a cloth dyed black or blue and decorated with cowrie shells. When Christianity was introduced, local dress was substituted for European dress and fabric.

However, later in the twentieth century, local adaptations and use of local fabrics and designs began to appear. A good example of these Yoruba changes is discussed by Elisha Renne (2000) who notes the shift in the way Yoruba textiles were regarded and the emergence of a new pride in being Nigerian. Nigerian values and identity were given new impetus, especially with the independence of the Nigerian state in 1960. Then in 1962, Vatican II allowed, and even encouraged, the previously disparaged cultural values of indigenous people (however, by this time no one was naked or scantily clad), and encouraged cultural diversity, including the use of locally produced textiles in ecclesiastical garments. Yoruba Christians added their own flavour to their vestments, incorporating locally produced, narrow strip handwoven cloth (*aso ofi*) in items such as the chasubles worn by Catholic priests and in the *aso ofi* habits worn by nuns. The current bishop, Bishop Fagun, now wears a range and combination of European and Yoruba dress: chasubles are made of *aso ofi* cloth with machine-embroidered religious themes such as St George slaying the dragon, thus combining tradition and modernity (Renne 2000).

Yoruba women religious continue to wear blue and white habits, but on one very special occasion, the ordination of young women as nuns, they wear handwoven *aso ofi* dress. At this particular Church ceremony, when they take their vows as brides of Christ, marking their transition from a worldly life to a religious one, they dress as Yoruba brides, wearing *aso ofi* blue and white wrappers, tops, and head-ties, embroidered in white, thus bridging the gap between their Christian and African identities through the subtle, but highly visible, medium of dress (Renne 2000:13).

Australian Aboriginal Anglican Clergy

Very early in the history of European colonization of Australia, representatives and missionaries of another Christian denomination, Anglicanism, settled in

Australia and began to spread their message to Aboriginal Australians. In north Queensland, the Reverend Gribble began to recruit Aborigines from various parts of Queensland and set up a mission station at Yarrabah, just south of Cairns. Several generations of Aborigines became Anglican Christians from the late nineteenth century through missionization.[10]

Though well-meaning, missionary enforcement of Christian morals onto Aboriginal people at Yarrabah mission, most of whom were brought there as small children from different tribal and linguistic groups, resulted in some humiliating practices for the mission occupants. Although boys and girls had segregated living quarters in dormitories, once attaining sexual maturity the inevitable occasionally happened: a girl became pregnant before marriage. At Yarrabah, this resulted in the couple being forced to marry in what was known as a 'ragtime wedding'. Before the wedding, they were made to have their hair completely shaved so that they looked bald, and to wear 'rags'. The couple was publicly shamed and not allowed any wedding festivities such as a 'spread' (wedding breakfast). Old people still remember this event with sadness and shame.

Mission superintendents maintained control of the mission until the 1960s when the Australian government took control. At this time, Aborigines could choose to attend or not attend church services, and many stopped going to church. With the disappearance of strict missionary control, alcohol problems began to surface, and many social problems escalated. Eventually however, some of the Yarrabah men turned to the Church and a few became Anglican ministers; one, Arthur Malcolm, even reached the status of bishop in 2001, becoming the first Aboriginal Australian to do so. His consecration as bishop was accompanied by the sound of the *didjeridu* and clapsticks.

As a bishop, Arthur Malcolm could select his own designs for his cope, the mantle or cloak that is worn over a cassock. The cope is individualistic to the degree that the design on each cope is selected by the particular priest to convey something which has personal meaning. Bishop Arthur Malcolm selected a design that reflects both his Aboriginality and the purpose of his ministry, to act as a bridge between the Aboriginal and white communities, and to reach out to everyone. His cope is embossed with a Christian cross, flames emerging from the cross, and a pair of upturned hands (one white, one black); underneath all this, is a boomerang with three crosses inside, reflecting the Christian themes of crucifixion and the Holy Spirit, and symbols of Aboriginality and his hope for the future. As a design, it was intended to depict the partnership of the two races which, as he stated, are 'one in Christ'.

Some of the Yarrabah Christian Youth group began wearing sweatshirts with a similar theme: a pair of hands, one black, one white, representing the hands of God reaching out to all people. The notions of the unity and equality of black and white people being brought about through Christianity is a recurring one among the Yarrabah Christians, as is the theme of the power of Jesus being able to equalize the two races and join them together through the love of God (Hume 1988).

Other Yarrabah clergy marked their distinctiveness from the European clergy by selecting Aboriginal symbols on their copes. One priest chose warrior motifs—spears, spear-throwers and boomerangs—because he wanted to emphasize fighting for the faith. Another chose 'benign' symbols such as a fish, a turtle and a lizard in traditional ochre colours. Yet another selected four boomerangs laid out in the shape of a cross, with an emu and a kangaroo above the cross and a crocodile below the cross. Another priest selected designs from a collection of north-east Queensland Aboriginal shields to convey 'defending the faith'. The traditional motifs on religious vestments, their coat of arms, and other clothing such as sweatshirts, also illustrates the proposed pan-Aboriginal nature of Christianity, as seen by these Aboriginal Christians (Hume 2010).

In the twenty-first century, the dress of Christians worldwide varies enormously and is always a reflection of history, politics and culture. Like clothing, jewellery and other embellishments vary, but the universal and principal symbol of Christianity remains: the cross symbolizing the crucifixion of Christ for the sins of humanity.

CROSSES, RINGS, ROSARIES AND *MEMENTO MORI*

The Christian cross consists of a straight line horizontally placed over a longer vertical line and is the Christian symbol par excellence. Its use in bodily adornment is ubiquitous, from explicit figures that depict a suffering, crucified Christ, to the highly abstract symbols of two simple crossed lines, any of which may be worked into pendants, necklaces, rings, earrings and bracelets that are simple and made of low-quality materials, to highly elaborate pieces that are inlaid with expensive rare gems.

Jewellery might include portraits of various popes and patron saints and medals associated with miracles. Pendants, necklaces, earrings, rings and bracelets could be engraved with a simple message such as 'Jesus', 'peace' or 'love'; longer phrases such as 'O Mary, conceived without sin, Pray for us who have recourse to Thee'; or a symbol such as a dove depicting the Holy

Spirit. Heart-shaped lockets sometimes opened to reveal an image inside, such as the Virgin Mary and Child, while men's Scapular rings had an image of Jesus in the centre with a cross and a heart.

With the basic themes around the biblical story of the crucifixion and the passion and kindness of Christ, there are a multitude of variations in jewellery in modern times. The beads that make up the rosary, which is particularly Roman Catholic, may be made from wood, bone, glass, crushed flowers, semi-precious stones such as agate, jet, amber or jasper or precious materials, including crystal, silver and gold.

The vast majority of modern-day rosary beads are made of glass, plastic or wood, and while the early rosaries were more likely to be strung on silk or other strong thread, contemporary rosaries are more often made as a series of chain-linked beads. Some prefer their rosary beads to be made of material with some special significance, such as jet from an especially holy shrine or sacred place. Beads might also enclose sacred relics or drops of holy water. The practical purpose of the rosary beads is as a counting device, to keep count of the number of 'Hail Marys' said, with the fingers moving along the beads as the prayers are recited in order to focus the mind more on the holy mysteries.

Mourning[11]

From the fourteenth to the early twentieth centuries, Christian jewellery was frequently engraved with the iconography of the *memento mori* (Latin for 'remember you must die'), such as a skull or a skull-and-crossbones, sometimes accompanied by words such as 'Live to Die, Die to Live'. Mourning rings, pins, fans and other commemorative objects were especially popular for both men and women in the eighteenth and nineteenth centuries and employed a variety of familiar symbols (skulls, urns, hourglasses, weeping willows) and phrases ('behold death', 'live to die' and *'memento mori'*).

Lockets, pins and rings could be inscribed with the deceased's initials and have a compartment which contained a lock of the deceased's hair. Pendants, brooches and rings might be shaped in the form of a coffin whose lid opened up to show the figure of a corpse within. Materials for making these items included silver, gold or enamel, sometimes encrusted with jewels. Mourning rings were popular between the sixteenth and eighteenth centuries. They were set with miniatures, human hair and precious or semiprecious stones; a family's coat-of-arms might be engraved on a ring, a locket or a pendant.

Christian mourning clothes in late nineteenth-century England were always black. Buttoned kid leather gloves accompanied a full floor-length dress, with pinched waist and long sleeves. Fabric for evening wear for those in mourning might include black net, tulle and Spanish lace, which could be purchased at shops or warehouses that specialized in mourning attire. Besides black gloves, a woman might add a black lace fan to her accessories. A full mourning bonnet in the 1890s might consist of bands of black crape (crepe) over a stiffened foundation, crape knot and semicircular black tulle veil over the face or behind the bonnet.

The public ending of the mourning period was usually marked by changing from black to other colours or by removing some outer garment, such as heavy neck decorations, one by one over time, allowing the mourner to be gradually reintegrated into social life.

The next chapter discusses the beliefs, practices and lifestyles of groups that greatly contrast with the hierarchical nature of the Roman Catholic Church discussed in this chapter. The focus is particularly on the Anabaptists, whose very foundations opposed all manner of richness in politics, dress and lifestyle, preferring instead to follow their Christian beliefs through an emphasis on simplicity in all aspects of living.

Simplicity and Humility: Anabaptist Orders of Amish, Hutterites and Mennonites

In contrast to powerful religious bodies with demonstrable opulence are those whose foundational belief structures are based on community, simplicity and humility, as well as isolation and conformity. Although we find such communities in the monastic orders within the hierarchical structures of large institutions, as we have seen in Chapter 1, there are communities whose very beginnings have opposed such hierarchy and whose foundations are based on a modest and humble communal lifestyle. Among these are the Anabaptists[1], whose three major groups are the Amish, the Hutterites and the Mennonites. The Anabaptists' set of rules for dress and behaviour indicate their preference for 'plain' dress, from dress style and colours to the prescribed way they do their hair, and their lack of any adornments. There is, however, still a small margin for resistance, and this is also played out in dress.

There are various levels of conservatism throughout the Anabaptist groups and this is played out visibly in dress. As of 2004, there were approximately 3,000 Amish, Hutterite and Mennonite communities in the United States alone, 65 per cent of whom dressed 'plain' (Arthur 2004). This chapter will focus on the more conservative communities, those who are called the 'plain people'. Their rules about dress and behaviour indicate their preference for simplicity, from style and colour, to the prescribed way they do their hair, and their lack of any adornments. With the emphasis on 'no frills', their plainness overtly articulates their separation from the world outside their communities and their strong sense of belonging and identity within their communities. There are variations even within the most conservative groups, however, and still a small margin for resistance, which is also played out in dress.

EARLY HISTORY

During the time of the Protestant Reformation in sixteenth-century Europe, some of the ideas held by small groups of the population were in opposition to those held by the powerful Roman Catholic Church. One of these ideas was the practice of infant baptism, and one of the most vociferous dissenting groups was the Anabaptists. Holding the belief that baptism was appropriate only for adults who were able to decide for themselves about their confession of faith, these groups were deemed radicals and soon were given the label 'Anabaptists' by their opponents (Kraybill 2008).

In 1525, Johannes Kessler wrote that the first Swiss Anabaptists 'shun costly clothing . . . expensive food and drink, clothe themselves with coarse cloth, [and] cover their heads with broad felt hats'. In 1568, the Strasbourg conference of Anabaptists decreed that 'tailors and seamstresses shall hold to the plain and simple style and shall make nothing at all for pride's sake . . . brethren and sisters shall stay by the present form of our regulation concerning apparel' (cited in Druesedow 2010:496).

The Anabaptist movement was sometimes called the Radical Reformation as its members openly debated with Protestant Reformers as well as Roman Catholic theologians. They wanted simple obedience to the Bible and the return to an early type of Christianity, pacifism rather than military service, and a focus on community, service and mutual aid. These dissenting radicals quickly spread through various parts of Europe, alarming civil and religious authorities who made concerted efforts to suppress them.

In Switzerland, re-baptizing adults became punishable by death, and in many parts of Europe, they were persecuted as heretics by burning them at the stake, drowning them in rivers, starving them in prisons or even executing them by decapitation. With the constant threat of execution and persecution, many moved into rural hideaways, but finding even this too dangerous, they eventually left Europe in the 1700s to make the long voyage with their families to the New World of North America, establishing communes in various regions. Anabaptist communities are now located in Pennsylvania, Ohio and Indiana, with some scattered groups in other parts of the United States as well as in Alberta and Ontario, Canada, and since the 1920s, Mexico.

The Amish and the Mennonites share a common Anabaptist heritage but divided into two distinctive communities in 1693. The Dutch Anabaptists gradually assumed the name Mennonite, from their Dutch Anabaptist leader, Menno Simons. The third of the major Anabaptist groups is the Hutterites, many of whom live in Canada.

While there is some diversity among Anabaptists as a whole, the 'plain people' all have similar approaches to simplicity: a plain style of dress and firm adherence to their community's rules, the *Ordnung,* a German word meaning order and regulations, which sets out explicit rules about all aspects of behaviour, both private and public, which are to be strictly followed after adult baptism. Avoidance of and separation from the outside world is crucial to their sense of community. Nevertheless, complete separation is not entirely possible, and there are times when the outside world impinges upon their isolation.

THE OLD ORDER AMISH

Amish people, named after their founder Jacob Ammann, are mostly scattered through Pennsylvania counties, with around half (57,000) living in Lancaster County (Kraybill 2008:2). They extend, however, to twenty-seven states and into Ontario, Canada. The Old Order Amish have resisted modern life by constructing cultural barriers around their community, drawing sharp boundaries between themselves and others. Their persistent use of horse and buggy instead of cars, lanterns instead of electricity, their very distinctive dress and their rules of behaviour distinguish them from the rest of North American society in a marked way.

The Old Order Amish communities are close-knit; they marry within their own kind and have limited interaction with outsiders. They prohibit higher education, preferring to educate their children in Amish schools on their own property, thus effectively raising them in the Amish way of life and insulating

Figure 2.1 Amish farmboys, Pennsylvania. Photo: Getty Images.

their young people from the influence of their non-Amish peers. They speak an old European dialect of Dutch or German, and they live a life of simplicity, only incorporating change if it does not disturb their way of life.

Nevertheless, they are constantly changing, and their willingness to compromise ensures that they do not die out. Change is minimal, however, and maintaining their way of life is of prime concern when introducing new ideas. For example, Amish are now allowed to ride in cars but not to own them; they can use phones and concede to having one telephone call box that can be used by the whole community when necessity calls for it, but they do not install telephones in their homes. Across Amish communities, these rules range along a continuum from orthodox to progressive: 'Low' churches observe strict discipline and are most technologically conservative, whereas 'High' churches are more relaxed. Despite this, all Amish communities are in touch with one other (Hamilton and Hawley 1999:31–52).

Dress Rules

As their dress reflects their foundational premise of a life of simplicity, there are strict rules about dress as there are rules for everything in Amish society. Community life is valued above the needs of the individual, and a quality that is deemed unacceptable is individual pride, *hokmut/hochmut*, a term that is used when someone tries to stand out from others. Pride disturbs the tranquillity of an orderly community, and individuals are expected to act without seeking personal recognition, which includes the rejection of fancy and gaudy decorations in the home or on the person, a definite indication of pride.

Clothing, household décor, architecture and mode of worship all reflect humility, simplicity, equality and orderliness. Cosmetics, jewellery, wristwatches and even wedding rings are not permitted as they are deemed to cultivate vanity, encouraging individuals to 'show off'. Whereas modern Western dress accents. individual expression and social status, plain Amish dress signals acceptance of the collective order. The opposite of *hokmut* is *demut*, humility, which is deemed to be a highly admirable quality. Humility, kindness and orderliness are sought-after individual attributes.

The women never cut their hair and all women wear their long hair in the same manner: in a bun at the back of their heads; a woman's loose hair is viewed as seductive so she never lets it out loose in public. Dresses are kept to a minimum number, with one dress being kept for Sunday best. Black stockings and shoes and modest eighteenth-century bonnets (fossilized fashion) complete the outfit. No jewellery is worn, and even visible pockets on

Figure 2.2   Amish mother and son, Pennsylvania. Photo: Getty Images.

dresses are not permitted. In Pennsylvania, the Amish stand out as being visibly and culturally different to everyone else in the surrounding environs in which they live, emphasizing their separateness.

Women wear clothing that is in every way modest, serviceable and simple: long dresses, the length of which is prescribed in the *Ordnung* ('not shorter than half-way between knees and floor, nor over eight inches from floor'), in solid, subdued colours (though these can be surprisingly varied, from a deep mulberry through to vivid pinks, purples and blues along with the more subdued black, brown and white); no bright red, oranges or yellow, and no ornamental or form-fitting immodest clothing. This extends to fabric such as silk or silk-like fabrics, so cotton and wool are preferred. Flat dress shoes have to be plain and black; no high heels are permitted. The matching aprons that are worn over the dresses indicate that they are always ready to work, and the entire dress indicates modesty. In the cold months, they wear black wool shawls, and layers of clothing underneath (Hamilton and Hawley 1999; Garrett 2003).

The vast majority of clothes are homemade, and some communities have their own shoemaker. Women in different Amish communities make their clothes from a range of dress patterns or styles. In 'Schumok' (a pseudonym used by Hamilton and Hawley (1999:40) to refer to a particular Amish community), the pattern dictates an open front bodice, elbow-length sleeves (or long sleeves in winter) and a fitted bodice with a narrow band-style collar. The bodice is attached to a same-fabric belt of about two inches in width to which the dirndl-type, centre-front-opened skirt is attached with a wide lap. The bodice is held closed by straight pins inserted horizontally down the front to the bottom of the belt. The skirt always comes to just below the knee on young girls and unmarried women but tends to be anywhere from two to six inches below the knee for married women, depending on their age. Colours vary, but those prescribed for married women in Schumok are quite dark in value and dull in intensity, in hues of burgundy, brown, navy blue and black. Unmarried girls are permitted to choose much lighter shades of rose, greens and blues (Hamilton and Hawley 1999).

A white organza prayer cap is worn by women inside the home, and when they move outside the home, they are expected to add the traditional eighteenth-century-style black bonnet over the cap. Subtle variations in caps and bonnets differ from one community to another. Girls in Lancaster County, Pennsylvania, for example, wear distinctive heart-shaped head coverings with a single pleat at the back (Scott 1986:100). Older women may wear white lawn bonnets, and their aprons are allowed to be brighter and lighter. Women also wear dark-coloured sweaters and capes, black hose and black shoes; however, unmarried girls and a few married women frequently go barefoot at home throughout the year. Amish women are expected to use no makeup.

The same clothing rules apply to children: the use of plain fabric in subdued colouring; children's dress mimics adult styles. As a young girl grows in stature and in size, the dresses that have been pleated to allow for growth are let out, demonstrating frugality and economy in all things.

To be concerned with fashion is to be disdainfully labelled 'worldly'. Men wear dark-coloured suits without lapels, high vests over homemade white or plain-coloured shirts, suspenders to hold up broad-fall trousers, black socks and shoes and a black felt or straw wide-brimmed hat. Their shirts fasten with conventional buttons and their suit coats and vests with hooks and eyes. Buttons are considered too ornamental, and fall into the category of *hokmut*, and zippers are deemed to be too modern. In Schumok, men wear heavy denim and a commercially manufactured man's dress shirt with sleeve length that depends on the season, leather-braided suspenders, a felt (winter) or straw (summer) hat and work boots (Hamilton and Hawley 1999:39). Men cut their hair in a 'Dutch bob', and wear beards after baptism or marriage, but not moustaches, as moustaches have long-term associations with the military, which they oppose (Kennett 1994)—along with a rejection of modernity, materialism and frivolity, they also reject war.

Homemade Clothing

Homemade clothing extends to wedding dresses that still follow traditional styles, but they are not white; rather they may be navy blue, sky blue or shades of purple. There is no fancy trim or lace adorning the wedding dress and never a train. Instead of a veil, the bride wears a white prayer cap on her head and an apron over her dress, indicating her readiness at all times for work even on her wedding day. There are no bouquets, and no one carries flowers. Following the ideal of practicality, the bridal dress becomes the woman's Sunday church attire after her wedding day. The groom and his attendants wear black suits and vests, white shirts, black shoes and socks, and as a special concession for the wedding, may wear small black bow ties. The groom's outfit is topped with a black hat with a three-and-a-half-inch brim. Both bride and groom wear black high-topped shoes. The ceremony is held in the bride's home.

While homemade clothing is considered more in line with Amish ways, a few items are purchased, being custom-made by special local 'English' (non-Amish) stores. Such items might be the women's bonnets, shoes, hats, stockings, underwear, men's everyday work shirts and winter coats. Acceptance of some change is seen in that some communities use a lightweight 100 per cent polyester knit for women's and girls' dresses, a fabric which is favoured for practical reasons: polyester dries quickly on an outside line or in a basement, a very useful quality in cold and wet climates when electric drying machines are not permitted. Twentieth-century synthetic fabrics are usually less expensive than natural fibres, and only the really conservative Amish shun synthetic fabrics (Hamilton and Hawley 1999). However, the rule of plainness prevails, and no printed textiles are allowed. Even wedding rings are not seen in an Amish community (Druesedow 2010). Commercially available products are used when they are seen to address their needs in a practical way without detriment to their basic rules.

What is visibly seen might sometimes hide some cheeky flaunting of the rules as Hamilton and Hawley (1999:41) discovered when they saw several pairs of bright, colourful men's boxer shorts with Disney characters on them on the washing line in a basement of an Amish house. Apart from the man's wife, nobody could see them and complain or gossip. In general, however, most Amish abide by the *Ordnung*, and rebellious acting up would be considered non-Amish behaviour; conformity is maintained through strong negative sanctions like gossip, and at worst, shunning, when an individual is completely ignored by the entire community.

Ruth Irene Garrett was raised in a strict Older Order Amish community in Iowa, but left in 1996. She was subsequently excommunicated. Garrett now devotes her time to helping Amish families who have left their communities. In her book *Crossing Over: One Woman's Escape from Amish Life*, she describes what constitutes modest clothing within a well-defined set of rules articulating conformity. Women's head coverings included 'starched organdy head coverings with eight pleats on either side. Not five or six pleats, but eight' (Garrett 2003:13).

Women were expected to wear head coverings all the time, including while they were asleep, she writes. Head coverings worn for attendance at church showed whether a woman was married or single: white for married women, black for single women. And hair must always be tied back in a bun. For working outdoors, women were permitted to wear scarves over their heads. There were also strict rules about shoes: they were to be lace-up, black leather shoes coupled with thick, knee-high nylon leggings. Dresses were to be no more than eight inches from the floor, and no display of bare skin was allowed except for the hands and face, though in summer, bare feet were permitted. Make-up was forbidden, as was shaving legs or under arms, fancy hairstyles, shoes with high heels and glittering jewellery (Garrett 2003:13).

Men, continues Garrett, dress in homemade buttoned cotton shirts that are often without pockets, zipperless denim pants that button in flaps across the front, suspenders, wide-brimmed straw or felt hats and black or brown boots. Men are not permitted to layer their hair or grow moustaches. Those who are married have beards; those who are single are clean shaven. Garrett also writes that the Amish order to which she belonged take great pride in restrained conformity. Their clothes represent their humility and their keenness to demonstrate the ideological trait of lack of vanity. They are more content taking their religious, agrarian life seriously, living by the motto that the harder it is on earth, the sweeter it will be in heaven. Such severity results in some insisting on wearing old and worn clothing, believing that this makes them 'more Amish'.

Sombre conformity extends to their horse-drawn buggies which also have to be kept plain: no long curtains in windows, no fussy decorations. The attention to plainness is also mirrored in a lack of expression. Excessive hilarity is frowned upon, and the Amish are said to rarely smile or laugh, though no doubt this was not always strictly the case. There are no photographs of people anywhere on Amish community properties (Garrett 2003:13).

Death

The rule of simplicity even follows through to death. A non-Amish undertaker moves the deceased to a funeral home for preparations with minimal cosmetic improvements. It is returned to its home in a simple wooden coffin within a day, and family members dress the body in white, symbolizing the final passage into a new and better eternal life. A deceased woman often wears the white cape and apron she wore at her wedding. This might differ according to the particular community. Scott (1986:84) writes that deceased men of the Holmes County Amish are dressed in their black suits and the women are dressed in black dresses.

There are no flowers, funeral cars or sculpted monuments. The hearse, a large, black carriage pulled by horses, leads a procession of other carriages to the burial ground on the property. A brief viewing and graveside service mark the return of the physical body from 'dust to dust'. Small, equal-size tombstones indicate the places of the deceased in a community whose members have all their lives lived with others in a sharing, communal environment. At death, as in life, the emphasis is on simplicity, and acceptance of what life may bring; there are no ostentatious displays for either the living or the dead: plain dress, plain living, and plain death. Bereaved women indicate their mourning by wearing a black dress in public settings for as long as a year.

There are slight variations in dress in other Anabaptist plain communities, but they all maintain the rule of simplicity. In Canada, the Hutterite women wear a polka-dot headscarf rather than a bonnet; the size of the dots indicate different communities. Their simple dress reflects both their religious beliefs and their insistence on a nonhierarchical community structure, with no central governance. Instead, there is a council of elders who make decisions for the community. Women's and men's roles, however, are quite specific.

THE HUTTERITES

The Hutterites[2] came from areas of the former Czechoslovakia, Hungary, Romania, Russia, Switzerland, Austria and south Germany and speak a distinct dialect of German known as Hutterite German, or Hutterisch, stemming from the sixteenth century. They fled Europe to escape religious persecution, making their way to North America to establish colonies and to follow their own communal way of life and religious practices, emigrating en masse to Canada in 1918. The majority live in the western provinces of Canada, namely Manitoba, Saskatchewan and Alberta, and have retained the simple austere lifestyle of their European ancestors.

The early Hutterites in Europe also refused to follow the Catholic and Protestant practices of infant baptism and state-run religion; consequently, they were persecuted and often killed for their strict obedience to their beliefs.

Under the initial leadership of Jacob Hutter, from whence derives their name, they established the basic tenets of Hutterian belief based on early Christian teachings and a strict separation of church and state (Hostetler 1997).

Although women are officially subordinate to baptized males in the colonies, have no voice in church matters and cannot hold leadership positions in the church colony policy, they have strong informal influence on colony life and hold managerial positions in the kitchen, kindergarten and some other areas. Their role is one designated traditionally as a woman's role, being responsible for cooking, medical decisions and selection and purchase of fabric for clothing. The wife of the (male) secretary sometimes holds the title of *Schneider* (from German 'tailor'), and she is in charge of making clothes and purchasing the colony's clothing fabric requirements.[3]

In spite of enormous changes in the world outside their own small communities, the Hutterite societies today have survived principally because of their uncompromising beliefs, their focus on community and mutual support rather than on individuals, their strict work ethic and their strategy to adopt only those aspects of the wider society with which they approve and that do not detract from their basic simplicity of lifestyle. Hutterites are highly disciplined and hardworking and practice frugality and communal sharing with no individual profit or gain.

Self-denial, humility, unconditional obedience and adult baptism are part of the righteous life dedicated to God. Fear of rejection or banishment is strong, which serves as a tight form of social control—one who sins excessively, is repeatedly drunk or is persistent in misconduct is 'cast out' of the colony. This is a severe form of punishment, as they believe there is then no hope of being accepted into heaven.[4]

Unlike the Amish, the Hutterites accept technological advances as long as they enhance the lifestyle of the colony as a whole and not individuals. No one in Hutterite society is poor or wealthy, and all receive their equal share in food, clothing, housing and care in old age. The world outside Hutterite colonies, that is the general North American way of life where individualism and capitalism are emphasized, is seen as based on greed and personal gain, considered by the Hutterites to be the epitome of carnality.

The communal distribution of goods in any Hutterite community is divided equally and in very specific amounts and types; for instance newly married grooms receive the following:

> one bed with mattress and pillow, a table and two chairs, a closet, cupboard, stove, wall clock, and sewing machine, and a set of Hutterite books; a bride receives from her colony seven yards and eight inches of bedspread material, ten

yards of comforter cover, material for a mattress pad sixty inches wide, six pillow cases, twelve yards of material for a feather comforter, an enamel dish, one cup and saucer, a kettle, spoon, knife, fork, soup pail, scissors, and a large chest. Clothing and bedding are homemade. (Hostetler 1997:191)

Following the general Anabaptist worldview, Hutterite dress not only empha-sizes modesty but also separation from the world. Clothes should not show vanity or pride in any way; instead, individuals should strive for inward beauty. There are differences of clothing styles among the various Hutterite groups, called *leuts*, but these differences, while significant to the Hutterites, may not be immediately noticeable to outsiders, as dress fundamentals remain the same. The men typically wear black or dark trousers held in place by black suspenders rather than belts, a black hat and a shirt of a solid colour. Gen-erally, the men's shirts are buttoned up with long sleeves and collars, and they may wear undershirts. Married men sport full beards, some with mous-taches (unlike some other Anabaptists), frequently topped by a cowboy hat for work and a plain black hat when attending church (Scott 1986:135–6).

The women wear ankle-length skirts or dresses with a blouse, a kerchief-style head covering with polka dots (*tiechle*), usually black and white, and solid comfortable shoes. The size of the polka dots on the *tiechle* indicates to which colony the women belong; the larger the dot, the more conservative; the smaller, the more liberal. Women often wear a vest over a blouse and a pleated skirt that may or may not match the vest. Fabrics may be floral, plaid or polka-dotted, sometimes matching their headgear, sometimes not (Scott 1986:72). Shoes and stockings are invariably black. Young girls wear their hair tucked under a bright, colourful bonnet (*mitze*) that fastens under the chin.[5]

Hutterites appear stoic in the highly practical clothes that give the appear-ance of a past era. In contrast to the plain look of the Amish and Old Order Mennonites, Hutterite clothing can be vividly coloured, especially on children. Most of the clothing is homemade within the colony. In the past, shoes were homemade but are now mostly store bought. The clothing worn for church consists of a plain dark or black long-sleeved jacket for both genders and a black apron for women. Men's church hats are always black.

Fashion trends do not figure in the Hutterite lifestyle, which has changed little in centuries. Clothing is not meant to please people, but to please God in every possible way. Covering or uncovering the head is cited in 1 Corinthians 11:4–5 which declares: 'Every man praying or prophesying having his head covered, dishonors his head. But every women who prays or prophesies with her head uncovered dishonors her head, for that is one and the same as if her head were shaved.'

Regional groups within the overall Hutterite community are further sub-grouped as the Lehrerleut, Dariusleut and Schmiedeleut, each one having slightly different dress styles. The Lehrerleut are considered to dress the most conservatively of the three, the Dariusleut slightly less conservatively and the Schmiedeleut the least conservative of the three. Lehrerleut women are recognized by the larger dots on their *tiechle*, while the Dariusleut women's polka dots are smaller, and the Schmiedeleut's *tiechle* either have no dots or else the dots are very small and far apart, giving a slightly different appearance to the *tiechle* of the other two groups of women.[6]

Dariusleut aprons are the same colour as their dress, while Lehrerleut aprons are a different colour and/or pattern. Schmiedeleut tend not to wear aprons. Children of all three groups usually wear lighter-collared clothes, and girls between the ages of about three to ten years wear a bonnet-like head covering called a *mitz*. It is important to note that particular dress styles are cultural traditions, and the goal is to wear modest and humble clothing. An individual who attempts to veer away from the accepted *leut*'s church ordinances is demonstrating pride, a quality that is much frowned upon, not only in Hutterite colonies but in all Anabaptist plain communities.

THE MENNONITES

Mennonites, the third major Anabaptist group, began arriving in North America in the eighteenth century, and their population is presently reckoned to be over a quarter of a million living in the United States. The Mennonites are the largest group among the Anabaptists, and plain dress is only to be found among approximately a quarter of the total Mennonite population (Arthur 2004). In the late nineteenth century clothing restrictions began to lessen among the Mennonites as they assimilated into the general American culture, accepted modern technology, and mingled with the rest of American society. By the 1980s, plain dress had been almost abandoned, in spite of a short revival between the 1920s and 1940s (Scott 1986:34). Those Mennonites who continue dressing plain are to be found in the most conservative communities, such as the Holdeman Mennonites (Church of God in Christ, Mennonite), described by Beth Graybill and Linda B. Arthur (1999), and the Old Order Mennonites.

Men's Dress

Mennonite men among the plain people may simply wear a plain suit, but no tie, to church, while at other times they tend to dress more like their non-Mennonite farmer neighbours in denim trousers and plaid shirts (Graybill and Arthur 1999). While the Amish and the Hutterites encourage a full beard (but generally no moustache), Mennonites are divided on this issue. In some groups men shave the face; in others a beard might be grown when the man is married or when the first child is born (Scottt 1986:108).

There are variations on the plain frock coat, long-sleeved shirt and vest; some men wear no tie, long ties, or bow ties. Trousers can be worn with or without suspenders and belt. Colours are black or sombre tones; shoes are generally black. Men's hats can be quite distinctive and serve to indicate a particular group of Mennonites. Many plain men wear hats with a plain crown and narrow brim, although others wear a wide brim (Scott 1986:131).

Women's Dress

Dress is more restrictive for the women than for men, highlighting gender segregation and placing the onus on women to maintain the tradition of plain dress (Arthur 2004). The man is seen as the head of the household and male power is a divinely ordained right—'God, man, woman. That's God's chain of command'—so while Anabaptist communities are opposed to the hierarchical nature of the large Christian institutions, the conservative groups nevertheless have a two-tiered system with relation to gender insofar as formalized authority is concerned (in Graybill and Arthur 1999:14).

The apostle Paul's instructions about women's dress are followed: women should adorn themselves in modest apparel, with sobriety, foregoing 'costly array' in favour of 'good works' (1 Tim. 2:9, 10), thus adhering to the Mennonite practice of shunning materialism and embracing practical work that is of benefit to a larger community rather than the needs of the individual.

The women in plain communities mimic the dress styles of their European forebears in earlier centuries, wearing dresses (never slacks or shorts) that are high-necked and loose, at least calf-length, and mostly with long sleeves. Some communities might choose subdued printed or patterned fabrics, others plain colours. To this might be added an apron and cape so as not to reveal body shape. The hair is pinned up in a bun at the back and covered by a black head covering (Holdeman communities) or white head covering (other conservative Mennonite communities). There is little or no ornamentation; no jewellery or cosmetics are permitted, and the cutting of hair is prohibited (Graybill and Arthur 1999). Until they reach puberty, young girls wear simple knee-length dresses, but upon the onset of puberty, a girl is expected to change to the style of all other adult women.

Group dress distinctions become notable through women's head coverings, from the small skullcap style with no ties that is pinned to the back of the head, through a range of full bonnets (see Scott 1986:128–33); fabrics may change according to seasons.

As there are rules for what *not* to wear, it seems that women may have attempted to deviate from the strict rules from time to time. It is stipulated that women must not wear 'loud colours or large print fabric patterns', add a large collar on a dress, or wear a dress that is too short, or add an extra trim or a wide ruffle on the sleeves. Even 'top stitching with contrasting thread' is not permitted, as it shows signs of 'pride' (Graybill and Arthur 1999:21). Some adaptations to modernity have been introduced. For instance, cotton fabric was used traditionally to make women's dresses, but when polyester came on to the market, it was adopted for women's dresses as it needed no ironing. Some fabrics (like organdy for bonnets) may have become too expensive to purchase (Scott 1986:43). Nevertheless, the patterns selected resemble the traditional calico styles in order not to draw attention.

However, there are some ingenious ways of getting around the prohibitions. While young women abide by the overall dress code, they use a snug fit or tucks, pleats, yokes and darts that help to accentuate a nubile female body, showing off their female sexuality during the years that they are looking for a husband. It is expected that a girl will be married by eighteen years of age, and certainly by the time she reaches twenty-one, at which time she is expected to conform to the behaviour of all other married women (Arthur 1998). Signs of individuality are seen to signify rejection of group norms and values and are frowned upon. One woman who left the church at the age of nineteen said:

> If your clothes are straight down the lines as to the rules of the group, then everyone can see that you are submitting your will to the Church. The Mennonite dress is like a uniform; it indicates that you're keeping everything under control. When you're having trouble with the [church's] rules, your clothing can show it. This is why everyone watches what everyone else is wearing and how they are wearing it, because clothing shows acceptance of all the rules of the Church. (Graybill and Arthur 1999:25)

As one woman said: 'When I put on Mennonite clothing, I put on all of the Church's rules' (Graybill and Arthur 1999:10). Conformity to dress, particularly the dress of women, is equated with religiosity among the conservative Mennonite groups and women are constantly observed for any disobedience to the rules. The outward appearance is considered to reflect the inner religiosity.

ANABAPTISTS AND CHANGE

However, subtle changes have continually occurred within all these communities.[7] One major modern change is that information about the Anabaptists is now easily accessible on the Internet and products made by them can be bought online. In addition, one can see numerous photos of all the Anabaptist communities on the Internet, whereas previously photos were never allowed to be taken of them.

As the Anabaptists grapple with the twenty-first century, mainstream technological changes and the rapidly changing world outside, one might expect that these communities would have a high rate of attrition and reduced numbers. However, the plain people are increasing in number as fertility rates continue to be high, and few are leaving their communities. The Amish population of North America increased from about 235,000 in 2008 to an estimated 282,000 in 2013. Amish continue to have large families and have managed to retain their young adults in spite of the lure of life outside. Among the Hutterite colonies, although some young people leave, most return; in 125 years their population has grown from 400 to around 42,000. The aggregate membership of the Mennonites is given as about 250,000, and Mennonite colonies have been increasing in numbers in Mexico since the 1920s.[8] It seems that, rather than diminishing, the number of Anabaptists is actually increasing.

It is interesting to reflect upon the 'plainness' principle in dress, as described in this chapter, and in the dress of the Roman Catholic women religious and the monastic orders of the Roman Catholic Church. 'Plainness' is a metaphor for simplicity and humility, while the wearing of ostentatiously rich fabrics, bright colours, precious gems and other embellishments visibly articulates power and prestige. Plainness and humility also seem to go hand in hand with bounded, cloistered and private communal groups that are not intent so much on proselytizing but on living a simple life and serving others or sharing labour and products within their own communities.

In the next chapter, two major monotheistic world religions, Judaism and Islam, will be discussed.

−3−

Fashioning Faith: Judaism and Islam

This chapter will look at two of the major monotheistic world religious traditions: traditional Judaism[1] and Islam. Codes of dress are specifically set out within Judaism; for example all leather worn must come from the skin of kosher animals, and the Torah forbids the mixing of linen and wool. In addition, there is a specific order for putting on clothes in preparation for ceremony or prayer. The dress of women and men are quite distinctive in Islam,[2] and there is much debate about the extent of bodily coverage with regard to the veiling of women. In both Judaism and Islam, there are separate areas for men and women within their respective synagogues and temples, setting them, visibly apart in their use of ritual space as well as in their clothing.

Within both of these religions, there are variations in dress between orthodox branches and the more relaxed progressive schools of faith, articulating that dress indicates differences not merely between different religions but also within the religions themselves. There are also very modern adaptations that push traditional boundaries but still remain loosely within them, and others that are rebellious and irreverent.

JUDAISM

Judaism is the religion of the ancient Israelites, whose origins purportedly go back nearly four thousand years (Maher 2006). Contemporary Jews are said to be the descendants of Abraham with whom, as stated in Genesis 17:1–14, God made a covenant that was to be kept throughout succeeding generations. As a sign of this covenant, all Jewish males must be circumcised, a practice which continues to the present day and is celebrated in the ritual of the bar mitzvah, when at age thirteen, a boy attains legal and religious maturity in the Jewish religion, committing himself to fulfil God's commandments. Thus, the modification of the body is the major physical sign of the covenant between God and all Jewish people.

Judaism is an all-encompassing way of life, and there are quite specific laws or standards for almost everything to do with the way one lives, including dress. Jewish law requires Jewish people to honour their bodies and to dress modestly, a quality that is repeated throughout all of the mainstream monotheistic religions. With the exception of the *tallith* and the *tefillin*, items of dress that are essentially the same for all Jews and which will be elaborated upon later, clothing customs vary from country to country (Ouaknin 1997:114), according to the particular branch of Judaism that individuals follow and the extent to which individuals wish to remain true to old traditions or leap with both feet into modernity.

The Five Books of Moses (Genesis, Exodus, Leviticus, Numbers and Deuteronomy), which according to tradition were given by God to Moses on Mount Sinai, make up the Torah. Torah study, which includes very specific dress codes that Jews must adhere to, is regarded as a religious duty for all Jews, and one of the most important liturgical acts in the synagogue is the reading from the Torah. The books of the Torah are written on scrolls made from parched or tanned leather and are to be found in all synagogues. As touching the scrolls with bare hands is forbidden, a pointer, called a *Yad*, in the shape of a finger or hand and usually made of silver or wood, assists the handling of the text during the reading (Ouaknin 1997 [1995]:42).

Jews observe the Sabbath, the seventh day of creation, ritually observed from an hour before nightfall on Friday to sunset on Saturday. Prior to this celebration, the house is cleansed, the meals cooked, the table set, baths taken and everyone in the family dressed for celebration (Ouaknin 1997 [1995]). The beginning of the Sabbath is marked by the ritual lighting of two candles. The menorah, a seven-branched candelabrum which is an ancient symbol of Judaism used in the Temple, represents Judaism as 'a light unto the nations' (Isaiah 42:6).[3]

The history of the Jews is a long one that is well covered in other writings (refer, for example, to Eric Silverman's *A Cultural History of Jewish Dress* [2013]). The destruction of the Second Temple in Jerusalem in the year 70 CE was a catastrophic time in Jewish history which brought on great changes in Jewish life. Jewish people lived and dressed in accordance with traditional Jewish law, *halacha*, but the rise and spread of Christianity, especially from the fourth century onwards, influenced the way that Jews were treated, and this extended to dress requirements imposed from without as well as from within. Old-style Jewish garb distinguished Jews from non-Jews and while socially detrimental in the wider world, it was viewed by the rabbis as a type of protection from the pollution of mixing with non-Jews (Silverman 2013). By the twelfth century, the despised Jewish minority in Europe and elsewhere were treated as the Other. This culminated in the Nazi epoch in the 1940s which forced Jews to be even more visibly other.

Figure 3.1   Jewish father and son lighting the nine-branched Hanukkah menorah. Photo: Getty Images.

Prior to the 1940s, however, in the moral, social and political changes of the New World of the Americas of the early 1900s, many Jews discarded pre-scribed traditional dress conventions and began to dress like everyone else. The chance to be fashionable in a high-consumer society provided them with the opportunity for individualism (Silverman 2013). Ultra-Orthodox Jews, how-ever, still clung to traditional dress as an outward sign of community, identity and Jewish values as some do even today.

The basic male garment for special ritual occasions is a *kittel*, a white, shroud-like linen gown that signifies purity, holiness, humility and new be-ginnings. The Jewish holy book, the Torah, forbids the mixture of linen and wool (specifically the wool of sheep, lambs and rams) in clothes. Although the reason for this is unknown, wool and linen attached to each other by any means, whether sewn, spun, twisted, glued or otherwise joined, is forbidden. However, it is permitted to wear a linen garment over a woolen garment, or vice versa, since they are not attached to each other. Traditionally, the first time a man wears a *kittel* is on his wedding day, then subsequently for Rosh Hashanah, Yom Kippur and Passover, and finally as his burial shroud.

Both single and married men wear a *yarmulke* (Yiddish), also known as a *kippah* (Hebrew), a small, embroidered or plain cloth skullcap in a variety of styles and fabrics, snugly shaped to the crown of their heads, demonstrating respect and reverence for God.[4] This item of clothing differs slightly, depending on the community. For example, in the Braslav communities (mystic Jews originating from Russia), the *kippah* is very wide, covering the whole head, and is usually embroidered, in a white or cream colour, and has a small pompon on the top (Ouaknin 1997 [1995]:118).

In Orthodox Sephardic communities (originating from Spain and Portugal), the *yarmulke* is embroidered but black, is smaller than the Braslavian *kippah* and is worn under a black hat. In Orthodox Ashkenazic communities of Germany or Eastern European origins it is also worn under a black hat but is made of black cloth. In non-Orthodox communities which accept modernity, it is embroidered and can be any colour (Maher 2006:114).

The Torah states no obligation regarding the wearing of the *yarmulke*, but it is a custom which has become obligatory through the passing of time and has become a sign of Jewish identity and of man's humility in his relationship to God. An Orthodox Jewish man may wear it all day because he believes himself to be in the presence of God at all times.

For morning prayers and at various religious ceremonies, men wear a prayer shawl (*tallith, tallis, tallit, talit*), a large rectangular wrap-around garment, which is traditionally woven of white wool, linen or silk, with black or blue stripes at the ends.

In the twenty-first century, the *tallith* is worn like a scarf and is sometimes pulled over the head to aid in concentration during prayer. Formerly, however, it was always wrapped around the head. When words, particularly those conveying the names of God, are inscribed upon physical objects of the world, these words are thought to send vibrations out into the physical world, and as the spirit of God is believed to pass through the *tallith* via the written word, a blessing is sometimes embroidered in Hebrew across the top of the *tallith*.

At each of the four corners of the *tallith* are the *tzitzith*, or fringes, in order to follow the commandment that man must be wrapped in fringed garments, made explicit in Numbers 15:37–40:

Figure 3.2   Three generations of Jewish men reading from the Torah. Photo: Getty Images.

The Lord said to Moses as follows: Speak to the Israelite people and in-
struct them to make for themselves fringes on the corners of their garments
throughout the ages. That shall be your fringe; look at it and recall all the commandments of the Lord and observe them. Thus you shall remember all My
commandments and to be holy to your God. I am the Lord your God, who brought
you out of Egypt.

And in Deuteronomy 22:12: 'you shall make yourself tassels on the four
corners of your cloak with which you cover yourself'.

Before wrapping oneself in the *tallith*, a blessing is said: 'Blessed art Thou,
O Lord, our God, Kingdom of the Universe, who has sanctified us by Thy commandments and hast commanded us to wrap ourselves in the fringed garments'. On some *tallith*, this blessing is embroidered in Hebrew across the
top of the shawl. In principle, the *tzitzith* should be made of the same material
as the *tallith*: a silk *tallith* should have silk *tzitzith*; a linen *tallith*, linen *tzitzith*
and so forth, but the most common practice is to use wool for the *tzitzith*, regardless of whether the *tallith* is made of wool.

Twined or knotted fringes or twisted cords (*tzitzith*) are affixed to the four
corners of the *tallith*, and each tassel has four strings (at least 1.5 inches
long); each corner has ten knots, which serve as reminders to the wearer
to keep the Ten Commandments. The number of times a thread is wrapped
around the others in the tassel corresponds numerically to the name of God.

There are different traditions of how to knot the *tizitzith*. Since they are considered by Orthodox tradition to be a time-bound commandment, they are worn only by men; Conservative Judaism regards women as exempt but not prohibited from wearing *tzitzith*. The fringes were attached to the outer garment with no attempt at or reason for concealment but due to later persecution, they became an inner garment, *tallith katan*, enabling the wearer to observe the Law clandestinely.

During the reading of a passage from the Hebrew Bible, the four *tzitzith* are held in the right hand and are kissed each time the word *tzitzith* is pronounced. From early childhood onwards, men usually wear a small *tallith* or a *tallith katan* under their clothes. Sometimes the ends of the *tzitzith* can be seen creeping out from under the shirt. The *tallith* is kept for life and even beyond; there is a custom of burying the dead in a *tallith*, after the *tzitzith* have been removed.

Another prescribed item of dress is the *tefillin*, worn by men during prayer, except on the Sabbath and on holidays. The *tefillin* consists of two long, thin leather straps, each one with a small leather box attached inside of which are tiny parchments, inscribed with texts from the Torah. One leather strap is worn on the left arm by wrapping the strap around it seven or eight times, and one is worn on the forehead positioned between the eyes, the strap being wound around the head and knotted. Both straps hang down over the shoulders. The single parchment for the arm bears four texts, while the four parchments for the head each bear one text: Exodus 13:1–10 and 13:11–16, and Deuteronomy 6:4–9 and 11:13–21. These items of dress are a form of both memory and memorial, allowing a man in prayer to become conscious of his ability to open up to the infinite, despite the finite nature of his material being.

Hasidic Jews

Hasidic Jews belong to one relatively small, but visibly apparent, branch of Orthodox Judaism which strictly adheres to the laws of the Torah, *halakha* (*halacha*), accepting that the Torah is divine revelation, regulating not only religious observance but also the entirety of the behaviour of its followers. The word *hasidim* translates as 'pious ones', reflecting their fervent passion for maintaining strict adherence to Jewish law. The *rebbe*, or master, is regarded as the spiritual intermediary between God and man; his interpretation of Jewish law is regarded as the paramount authority in a Hasidic community, as he is believed to possess a higher soul than others. Each Hasidic community is directed by its own *rebbe* and his interpretation of Jewish law (Carrel 1999).

The Hasidic movement began in the eighteenth century in Eastern Europe, and consequently, much of their distinctive dress and hairstyle are based on clothes worn by the nobility of eighteenth-century Poland and other places in Europe. Atop either black or very dark clothing, the most strikingly visible part of male dress which sets them apart from others is their hair, worn in long side curls, called *payos*, which hang conspicuously in front of the ears, though the rest of the hair may be cut short. Some men wear traditional dress only on the Sabbath and holy days, but others dress in this way every day. All males are required to wear a head covering to show respect for God, a reminder that there is a creator, a higher power, above humans. In Hasidic communities, a fur-trimmed hat called a *streimel* is common.

Because of the importance of the *rebbe*, the Hasidic top-ranking religious leaders, the *rebbes'* clothing consists of the most highly valorized signs of the Hasidic men's dress code. They are the only ones who wear the *shich* and *zocken* (slipper-like shoes and white knee socks), the *shtreimel* and *bekecher* (fur hat and long silk coat), *kapote* (overcoat), *biber* (large-brimmed hat) and *bord und payes* (beard and side locks) (Ouaknin 1997 [1995]:114). Individuals who are not *rebbe* but consistently display intense religious observance, a gradual process affected by increasingly religious behaviour, can be invited by the *rebbe* to wear such elaborate clothing to demonstrate their commitment to the faith. A person who wears extremely Hasidic clothing would be ridiculed if his behaviour were not consistent with his appearance (Carrel 1999:169).

Jewish mystics ascribe esoteric significance to the beard, and, according to Scripture, it is forbidden to cut the corners of a man's beard (Lev. 19:27). Among European Jews, the emphasis shifted from the obligation to wear a beard to the prohibition of shaving. However, it is permitted to clip the beard using scissors or an electric shaver with two cutting edges.

Women and Modesty

In general, within Judaism, both men and women are advised to dress modestly and both must cover their heads in the synagogue and when in prayer in reverence for God. Women often dress in white on special ritual occasions. A Jewish bride often wears white, but it is not obligatory. Before the ceremony, the bride is veiled in remembrance of Rebecca, who veiled her face when she was brought to Isaac to be his wife (Ouaknin 1997 [1995]:128). The white wedding dress signifies purity and her new beginning as a married woman, but in general, the expectation for women is only that they dress modestly, adhering to the laws of *tzniuth*. Laws concerning clothing and appearance derive from two sources: the *Dath Moshe*, or those requirements specified in the Torah itself, and the *Dath Yehudith*, or varying written traditions which have defined the practice of Jewish women through generations by means of community interpretation (Carrel 1999).

Just as a Torah-observant man's skullcap or hat is required to cover his head, a woman's head covering (wig, hat, scarf or any combination of the three) is believed to serve the same purpose. While single women and girls may leave their hair uncovered, married (and formerly married) women are required to cover their hair entirely:

> What is the particular mark of the married woman's modesty? She covers not only her body, but the hair of her head as well. A woman's hair is lovely. Reserved for her husband's eyes, her loveliness is sacred, in keeping with the laws of modesty. (Ki Tov 1963:77)

The long hair of a woman is considered erotic, a theme found throughout various religions, across cultures, and even in Hollywood movies, a universal feature which commonly depicts loose flowing hair as being the mark of the loose woman. In Judaism, just as in many other religions, hair is considered to be a very sensual part of a woman's body; it is a symbol of her 'libidinal energies' (T. Turner 1980:114). Certainly, long, abundant hair allowed to fall loosely has always been depicted as a sign that a woman is as loose in her morals as the hair falling down her back. Hollywood has made much of this idea. Some rabbis compare the exposure of a married woman's hair to the exposure of her private parts.

As in other strict religious approaches to the triad of women, dress and modesty, the appropriate clothing for women in Hasidic law is inseparably bound to modesty, or *tzniuth*, and applies to women of all ages. There has been a long history of the interpretive struggle to construct an appropriate embodied representation of *tzniuth* and Hasidic womanhood (Carrel 1999:166). Modesty in dress leads to women being restricted from wearing any form of trousers or slacks in some communities.

Strictly speaking, the Torah forbids a married woman to appear in public without her hair covered, and when taken literally, if a woman disobeys this ordinance, her husband has grounds for divorce and her dowry is forfeited, as her hair is supposed to be reserved for her husband's eyes only. Hasidic women make every effort to follow this ordinance for hair covering, and in some Hungarian sects, women either shave their heads completely or closely crop their hair following the wedding ceremony, ensuring that not one hair will be seen even unintentionally.

In the Middle Ages, married women cut or shaved off their hair, covering their heads with kerchiefs. Some women wore, on the forehead, a facsimile silk band known as a *schpitzel* (brown pleated material) or front piece as a substitute for the colour of their hair. At the end of the eighteenth century, some Jewish women began wearing wigs as their primary manifestation of head covering (Carrel 1999:171).

The Torah-observant Jewish man's skullcap or hat covers his head, while a woman's head covering, whether it is a wig (*sheytl*), hat, scarf (*tikhl*) or any combination of the three, is believed to serve the same purpose in addition to serving as a symbol of modesty and marriage (Carrel 1999:166). Head coverings, particularly those that reveal no natural hair whatsoever, are the quintessential symbol of Hasidic womanhood, followed by leg coverings and appropriate length of skirt. Women's head coverings within Hasidic Judaism symbolically display a hair hierarchy of orthodox modesty, from those deemed 'most religious' to those deemed 'least religious': absolute absence of any display of hair is at the top of the category of 'most religious'. The woman who wishes to show that she is extremely religious has her hair completely hidden under a *tikhl* (Carrel 1999:166).

Following this is hair covered by the *tikhl* but with the addition of a *schpitzel*, a piece of brown pleated material that feigns the appearance of hair. A 100 per cent synthetic hair wig demonstrates a more religious woman than one who wears 50 per cent synthetic hair; and a woman who wears a wig made of human hair is considered to be much less religious than the aforementioned. They are, however, all religious because their natural hair is covered by a wig. Wigs that look like natural hair are viewed with suspicion.

While the wearing of the wig became popular for a time with all Jewish women, it now marks the women of the Orthodox Jewish community, when it is worn as a head covering rather than a fashion statement. Most American Jewish women no longer wear a head covering of any kind. The *sheytl* and *tikhl* have become the symbol of the Torah-observant woman, both the traditional Orthodox woman and the Hasidic woman.

According to Jewish law, *ervah* is the term that implies erotic stimulus, and a woman's hair, along with several other parts of a woman's body, is *ervah* (Fuchs 1985). Other areas include her neck (below and including the collar bone), her arms (the upper arms, including the elbow) and her legs (the thighs, including the knees) (Carrel 1999:165). Hasidic women's dress and appearance are specifically regulated by *halakhoth*, or laws of the Torah, to ensure that *ervah* parts are covered. The many *halakhoth* that define appropriate clothing and presentation for an observant Jewish woman are inseparably bound to *tzniuth*, or modesty, the guiding principle for all Hasidic women, young and old. One *halakhah* states that it is a serious transgression for an observant Jewish woman, through clothing or appearance, to follow the ways of the non-Jew or nonobservant Jew. To be truly Hasidic, one should not desire fashionable dress.

Modernity

Today, American modern Orthodox Jews, with ideas of change stemming from the mid-nineteenth-century religious modernization movement, take a different approach to dress. Young Jewish adults might demonstrate their Jewish identity in somewhat rebellious ways, transforming Jewishness 'from a religious and historical heritage into an ethnic identity that is hip, sexy, and cheeky' (Silverman 2013:491). The traditional nonleather shoes worn at Yom Kippur might appear as canvas sneakers or colourful plastic Crocs, and women may be seen in the synagogue in previously forbidden pantsuits or slacks or even hot pants and miniskirts.

Jewish clothing, suggests Silverman (2013), 'expresses unresolved yet open-ended conversations about Jewish identity'. The 'New Jew Cool', a 'hip-hop style of Jewishness', is one of the latest to enter this conversation. North American pop culture has influenced styles of yarmulkes, and there are names that show this new trend such as 'KoolKipah', 'Lids for Yids', and character names from pop culture. Modern Orthodox Jews tend to wear small, colourful knitted or suede yarmulkes, often fastening them on with a bobby pin or a 'kippah clip'. Even the placing of the yarmulke on the head conveys meaning: the more tradition oriented place it more toward the front of the head, whereas the more liberal wearer places it toward the back of the head (Silverman 2013).

Women have asserted their right to wear fringed prayer shawls in the synagogue, demonstrating both their commitment to Judaism as well as feminism (Emmett 2007). Prayer shawls that women wear might be 'made from silk, hand painted with pastel colors' and often display images of flowers (Silverman 2013). A woman might also personalize her prayer shawl, having it made from a wedding dress or a deceased relative's neckties.

In the twentieth century, girls began to be included in the ritual of maturity that was previously only a celebration for boys. Some of the more Orthodox communities still reject this celebration for girls however. For the important rituals of circumcision (the *bris*), merchants now offer special *bris* garments that allow for circumcision to be performed on boys with less hindrance from clothing. Instead of the trousers normally worn, the white suit tops sit atop a skirt-like lower half. No prescribed dress is worn by the girls (Tortora 2010:486).

Death

While mourning practices are extensive within Judaism to show respect for the dead and to comfort the living, death is regarded as a natural process and a part of God's plan. When a person dies, the eyes are closed, the body is laid out and covered, and someone keeps vigilance over the body until burial. A window in the room where the deceased passed away is usually opened so that the *neshamah* (soul) can escape as soon as possible.

The presence of a dead body is considered a source of ritual impurity, so anyone who has been in the presence of a corpse must wash their hands before entering a home whether or not they have physically touched the body. The corpse is thoroughly cleaned and wrapped in a simple, plain linen shroud (*tashrichim*), and may also be clothed in the deceased person's *tallit*, the *tzitzit* having been removed beforehand. The body is not embalmed, must not be cremated and is never displayed in an open casket, something which is considered disrespectful. At the appropriate time, it is placed in a plain and simple coffin, ready for burial in the earth. Traditionally, Jewish corpses do not generally undergo embalming or cosmetic restoration, although some Jewish families may select these procedures (Bank 2005:68–9).

The ritual of *Keriah* (tearing one's garments) is performed by mourners (Ouaknin 1997 [1995]) either before the chapel service or at the graveside service, as a display of separation. The garments may also be torn immediately upon hearing of the death of a loved one or the mourner may wear a black ribbon on their clothes. Certain practices are carried out, such as covering all the mirrors in the house, refraining from wearing leather shoes, avoiding washing clothes or wearing new clothes, and avoiding bathing, shaving and cutting the hair or nails.

Jewish Jewellery

The Star of David, or the *Magen David*, is a major symbol which figures on clothes as well as jewellery. Bracelets, more often worn by women, but also by men, might show specifically Jewish symbols such as the *Chai*, the *hamsa*, and the Star of David, among others. The *Chai* is from the Hebrew related word *chaya*, meaning 'life' or 'living thing', a combination of the two Hebrew letters *Cheit* and *Yod*. Some say it reflects Judaism's focus on the importance of life. A Jewish toast is *l'chayim* ('to existence'). An entire symbol such as the *Chai* might be made of crushed opals, set in gold, on a gold chain and worn as a pendant (Ouaknin 1997 [1995]).[5]

The *hamsa* is a stylized hand with the thumb and little finger pointing upward showing the five digits, said to represent, for Jews, the five books comprising the Torah. It is an ancient Middle Eastern amulet symbolizing the Hand of God and can be found in many faiths throughout the Middle East and Africa to symbolize protection, happiness, health and good fortune. It is also called the Hand of Miriam, named for the sister of Moses. Arab culture refers to this symbol as the Hand of Fatima. The *hamsa* hand is a symbol that is used in both Judaism and Islam. Bracelets that are shipped throughout the world from Israel and other places via the Internet include a gold plate or silver *Chai* attached to a black leather cord, a sparkling *hamsa* on a gold-plate disc attached to a red leather cord, or a leather cord with multiple symbolic charms such as a pair of shoes, a *hamsa*, a peace symbol or a heart.[6]

Necklaces might have any of the above symbols, as well as a *Ben Porat Yosef*, words that signify a prayer against the evil eye, some with the letters ALAD on one side of a rectangular shape, often in gold or silver, and the words *Ben Porat Yosef* on the other side. Gems such as turquoise, crystal, diamonds and sapphires, among others, might be inlaid on any jewellery.

Gold or silver wedding rings might bear Hebrew phrases from the Song of Songs, such as, 'I am to My Beloved as He is Mine' (*Ani Ledodi Vedodi Li*). Biblical motifs such as the Mezuzah, the ancient Jewish symbol for good luck and Jewish identity, and the words *El-Shadai* (God all mighty) from Deuteronomy 6:9 and 11:19, referring to the words that are often written on house doorposts or gates as a reminder of God's presence, may figure on pendants. Like jewellery in all traditions there are a multitude of combinations of symbols and materials that are used.

Israeli artist David Weizman creates pieces that reflect spiritual elements of the Jewish tradition that are meant to inspire the wearer and bring health and happiness. His Kabbalist training shows up in jewellery that depicts the Kabbalist Tree of Life, a symbol of the *Sefer Yetzira* (Book of Creation) with its ten *sefiroth* and the twenty-two letters combining to form the thirty-two 'paths of secret wisdom'.

ISLAM: FROM THE BURQA TO THE BURQINI

The strictly monotheist religion of Islam began in the Arabian peninsula with the Prophet Muhammad, born circa 570 CE, who is said to have been visited by the angel Gabriel in the year 610 CE, a powerful experience that transformed his life and convinced him of his prophetic call. Muslims believe that Muhammad is a prophet of God: 'There is no god but Allah and Muhammad is his prophet'.

The Qur'an, Islam's holy book formed between 610 and 632 CE, contains the compilation of revelations communicated to Muhammad by the angel Gabriel. It contains 114 *surahs*, or chapters, and more than 6,000 verses. As in all sacred texts, interpretation, which carries on into belief and action, is fundamental to how the meanings of the texts are perceived. Some interpretations are liberal and metaphorical; others tend towards fundamentalism and literal interpretations of the sources. The *Hadith*, composed of the words and actions of the Prophet Muhammad, and the actions and words of others in the presence of Muhammad, all of which were accepted by Muhammad, is separate to the Qur'an, but highly important to all Muslims.

Each Muslim is deemed to be personally accountable to God, expected to submit to God's teachings, and to surrender his or her will to the Will of God, following the Shari'ah, the sacred law of Muslims, and according to the five Pillars of Islam: (1) profession of faith: 'There is no god but Allah and Muhammad is his prophet'; (2) observance of the call to prayer at five specific times per day, facing towards Mecca, in Saudi Arabia; (3) almsgiving, or tithing, to help the poor and needy; (4) abstinence from all food, water and sexual activity from sunrise to sunset during the entire month of Ramadan; and (5) pilgrimage to Mecca, the holiest of all Muslim cities, at least once in a lifetime. The Shari'ah contains teachings and practices for everything concerning Muslim life, a code of behaviour which dictates what is permissible and what is forbidden.

Like all religions that are exported to foreign cultures, Islamic orthodoxies have been influenced by local folk customs. For example, many Muslims in Pakistan and Nigeria use charms to ward off evil, and in parts of Afghanistan and India, Muslims hang strands of hair at shrines to protect their children. In Sudan, the local Muslim leader might also be a medicine man who uses local tribal customs to keep Satan away. Muslims in many Islamic countries may use magical objects to keep from being hurt by the evil eye (Melton and Baumann 2002:686).

Revivalist trends during the past two centuries, expressed in moderate and extreme Islamist movements, have created an intense focus on the Islamic world from outside the religion, and an international focus on the role and position of women with an emphasis on the thorny issue of veiling, about which there has been enormous academic and public debate.

Islamic responses to all this have varied, and played out to quite a large extent through the insistence on specific forms of dress, especially that of women. In some areas, strict codes have been enforced on the way women dress, and in others, it is the woman's choice. Muslim women in Turkey and Palestine have voluntarily re-veiled as an outward expression of their anti-Western sentiment, and what they see as the loose morals of Western society, an idea that is reinforced by photos of scantily clad Western women and increasingly lax mores in Western society.

The Qur'an calls on both women and men to be modest and to guard their modesty in public (Khuri 2001). A Muslim man must always be covered from the navel to the knees and should not wear tight, revealing or eye-catching clothing. The term 'veil' becomes ambiguous when comparing an item of dress that covers the face across a number of different Islamic cultures. While there has been much emphasis on the veiling of women, Fadwa El

Guindi (1999) points out that in some cultures, and at different epochs, both women and men may wear head and face covers.

The Prophet Muhammad 'face-veiled' on certain occasions (El Guindi 1999:117). The Arabic term *lithma* is used for a dual-gendered face cover; when worn by women in Yemen, it is associated with femaleness, but when it is worn by Bedouin and Berber men, it is associated with virility and maleness (El Guindi 1999:7). The Tuareg men wear a cloth that is wrapped around the head to form a turban, with the end being brought across the face, sometimes showing only the eyes, sometimes the eyes and nose. A noble Tuareg man does not expose his mouth; a covered mouth communicates his rank and

Figure 3.3 Muslim woman praying in a mosque. Photo: Getty Images.

respectability, and a man's veil is also a mark of maturity, and thus not worn by boys (El Guindi 1999:123–6).

The specific passages in the Qur'an (in the chapter *Nur* XXIV:31) that relate to veiling call on women to 'draw their veils over their bosoms', and 'not display their beauty' except in the presence of their husbands, their fathers, their husbands' fathers, their own sons, their husbands' sons, their own brothers, their brothers' sons, or their sisters' sons (Khuri 2001).

There is nothing in the Qur'an that indicates a dress code of complete veiling, however concealing and revealing the body are tied to cultural notions of respectability, sexuality, eroticism and privacy. Both men and women are responsible for maintaining the sanctity and reputation of the family. Veiling is about identity, kinship, rank, class, sacred privacy and sanctity. The veil links worldly and sacred life, and there is a link between 'dress, women and the sanctity of space', says El Guindi (1999:136).

The Body

As the body is viewed as a gift from God, men as well as women are expected to be impeccably clean and, in general, much care is given to having a meticulously clean appearance. A filthy appearance is anathema to Muslims. Cleanliness is expressed by keeping the body clean, the fingernails well polished, the teeth 'well kept' and, for men, the beard well trimmed (Khuri 2001:30). All bodily secretions—urine, blood, menstrual blood, faeces, vomit and semen—are regarded as pollutants. Although the body is a gift from God, it is also a potential source of shame and therefore needs to be concealed and covered. This applies equally to men and women.

For all Muslim males, whether Sunni or Shi'ite, clerical or lay, the wearing of gold or silk is forbidden in consequence of a prescription of the Prophet. Because covering the head is a Near Eastern way of showing respect, a head covering should properly be worn in a mosque and even when praying outside the mosque. In order not to defile the mosque, footwear must be removed on entering in case ritually impure substances have adhered to the sole of the shoe, a rule which also applies to entering a graveyard; thus, gravediggers and stonemasons must be barefoot on such occasions.

For all Muslims, the standard grave clothes are the threefold linen shroud, or *kafan;* the *izar*, or lower garment; the *rida'*, or upper garment, and the *lifafah*, or overall shroud. Martyrs, however, are buried in the clothes in which they die, without their bodies or their garments being washed because the blood and the dirt are viewed as evidence of their state of glory. When a person shows signs of dying he or she is usually positioned on his or her back with the feet facing Mecca and allowed to rest in a room that is devoid of anything that is regarded as 'unclean', such as a menstruating woman, and the room is perfumed. Appropriate passages of the Qur'an are recited by the dying person, or if the person is unable to do this, a relative will do it for them. The dying person is expected to repent of his or her sins and to recite the basic creed of Islam: 'There is no God but Allah and Muhammad is his Prophet'. Immediately upon death, the mouth and eyes are closed, feet are tied together and the body is covered with a sheet. The body is gently cleaned, perfumed and wrapped in white cotton by members of the family. The deceased is then placed in a plain wooden coffin and carried to the place of burial where it is taken from the coffin and lowered into a six-foot-deep grave. It is then covered with flowers and dirt, and rose water that has been blessed is poured over it. The mourners are reminded that all humans are made from dust and return to dust.

The discrepancy between men's and women's bodies becomes more apparent in the conditions Islam stipulates for prayer, which includes, among other things, a state of purity, clarity of intent, facing Mecca, and covering the body. These conditions are equally required from men and women.

Pilgrimage

When a Muslim man dresses for the major pilgrimage (*hajj*) to the holy city of Mecca, in Saudi Arabia, he robes himself in two white seamless garments (*ihram*), which may not be exchanged for normal dress until he deconsecrates himself after the conclusion of the pilgrimage ceremonies. There is prescribed dress code for both men and women during pilgrimage as well as during prayer. Women must cover themselves from head to toe, with the exception of the face and hands. Men must cover themselves from the navel to the knees. In preparation, both must purify themselves through ritual cleansing, and following certain ritual procedure such as cutting fingernails and toenails, removing unwanted body hair, trimming beards and moustaches and washing and combing the hair along with recitations. The body must be fully purified by water before donning white clothing (both men and women) (Vogelsang-Eastwood 2010). Men are not to wear *kamis* (upper shirt), pantaloons, hooded cloak, or sewn footwear. For men, ordinary dress is replaced by an *izar*, consisting of two unsewn wraps that extend from waist to feet, as well as a covering over one shoulder and the upper body, known as the *rida'*. While a woman's hair and head are covered, she does not wear a face veil. Women and men refrain from wearing both perfume and jewellery.

Many women in the twenty-first century choose to wear an international form of *ihram* consisting of a white dress worn with a garment called a *khimar* that covers the head, shoulders and upper body that gives the appearance of a large hood (Vogelsang-Eastwood 2010). Having performed a pilgrimage, a man receives the title of *hajj*, a woman the title of *hajja* (El Guindi 1999).

In Sura 70:4, it is written: 'Say to the believing women that they should lower their gaze and fortress their *farj* that they should not display their beauty and ornaments except what [ordinarily] appear thereof'. The term *farj* refers to nakedness and genitalia, and the phrase 'fortress their *farj*' means to guard one's chastity; to be clean, modest and chaste. For women, this also implies preserving virginity, 'drawing their veils over their bosoms' and refraining from 'tapping the floor to draw attention to their hidden ornaments' (Sura 24:31). In Sura 16:2, it is written: 'Say to the believing men that they should lower their gaze and fortress their *farj*; that will be more fitting of them. And God is well acquainted with all that they do.'

With regard to the lowering of the gaze, men are not to stare at people or look them in the eye, rather they should look sideways or downward, which signifies politeness and humbleness. For men and women who fortress their *farj*, God has prepared forgiveness and great reward in the afterlife (Sura 15:29) (Khuri 2001:30).

Touch, Sound and Perfume

Touch and sound are other aspects of sexuality which Islamic jurists have discussed in some detail. Even seemingly simple and innocent gestures such as shaking hands, touching shoulders or any other form of body contact between the sexes can be viewed as very inappropriate (Khuri 2001). In Islam, it is forbidden for a woman to shake hands with a man other than an immediate family member, especially if she has fulfilled the duty of pilgrimage. Customarily, however, many women cover their hand with a scarf while shaking hands with a friend. While clothing may mask the body and veil the face, it does not hide the sounds that emanate from the body, drawing attention to it, such as the tapping of feet, the rattling of any items of clothing or other dress such as anklets, or the clicking sound of high-heeled shoes. Islamic morality is not against men's and women's sexuality, rather it is the public flaunting of sexuality which is abhorred. Drawing public attention to sexuality by the way one dresses or moves is viewed as exhibitionist behaviour.

The Prophet Muhammad commented favourably on the use of tattoos and ornamentation of kohl around the eyes, which he particularly liked; he is noted to have remarked: 'I do not like to look at women with no tattoos on her hand and no kohl on her eyes' (Khuri 2001:80). Concerning smell, the Prophet repeatedly encouraged Muslims to use perfume. While restrictions apply to the outward visible appearance of women, restrictions are rarely placed on perfumes. In one of his famous *hadiths* on the subject, he said: 'Two things in this world earned my love and affection, women and perfume', making it clear that perfume is a respectable and desirable facet of dress (Khuri 2001:82).

Within the enclosures of the Moroccan harem in which Fatima Mernissi, the Moroccan feminist writer and sociologist, was born and raised, the women would dress up in their most cherished caftans and, sitting in a quiet corner of their salons,

> put some musk, amber, or other fragrance onto a small charcoal fire, and let the smoke seep into their clothes and long unbraided hair. Then they would braid their hair, and put on kohl and red lipstick. We children especially loved those days because our mothers looked so beautiful then, and forgot to shout orders at us. (Mernissi 1994:237)

Her aunt would say to her:

> Beauty is in the skin! Take care of it, oil it, clean it, scrub it, perfume it, and put on your best clothes, even if there is no special occasion, and you'll feel like a queen. If society is hard on you, fight back by pampering your skin. Skin is political. Otherwise why would the *imams* order us to hide it? (Mernissi 1994:238)

There was also a whiff of magic in the making of the home-made cosmetics, hair washes and creams produced by the women of Mernissi's harem. They would mix their 'mysterious plants and flowers in secrecy', fragrant plants like lavender, myrtle, rosebuds that had been collected from the countryside by the men of the family. Kilos of dried roses and myrtle were among the ingredients used, the dried flowers put in pots and left to simmer slowly.

Some women 'dried their roses in the moonlight' and recited magic incantations over their plants to enhance their enchanting powers (Mernissi 1994:248). Women and men purified themselves separately in a series of bath chambers. Purification rituals prior to preparing for prayer took place in these chambers, care being taken to wash body parts in strictly prescribed order and in silent concentration: first hands, then arms, face, head, and finally the feet.

Arab Muslim women perfume their bodies and clothes with many kinds of scents, including aloe wood, musk, ambergris, gum Arabic, rose and sugar, as well as any commercial brand of perfume on the market. Fragrance is often closely identified with beneficial deities and forces, while foulness is associated with harmful ones. Muslim inhabitants of the United Arab Emirates, for instance, say that 'a dirty, smelly body is vulnerable to evil', while the scented person is 'surrounded by angels' (Classen, Howes and Synnott 1994:130).

The most efficacious scent for attracting angels and dispelling evil spirits is thought to be frankincense smoke. Both scented oils and incense are employed in adding fragrance to clothes; after clothes have been washed and dried, they are placed on a rack over an incense burner until completely covered and all the fragrant smoke is absorbed by the material. The smell can stay in the clothing for at least three washes, and the fragrance might be intensified by incensing them more frequently. A censer might also be used under the veils to perfume the hair and face as well as the clothing (Classen, Howes and Synott 1994:128).

Nevertheless, any behaviour in public that draws attention to the woman and that might arouse the olfactory and auditory senses of men, which includes the wearing of perfumes and the noise of ankle and wrist bracelets, as well as the visual allure of finger nail polish and make-up, are considered unacceptable in some areas.

Women and the Veil

A wide variety of head coverings shapes and forms are worn by women in Islamic communities throughout the world, varying mostly in accordance to the interpretation of what 'veiling' means and what female modesty dictates in different cultures. In addition to culture, other factors affecting the wearing of the 'veil' are ethnic group, geographic region and even rural and urban locations. While face, head and body coverings follow prescribed rules, there are a multitude of cultural and personal variations on how this is done. The veil is a generic term used universally, but especially by Westerners, to refer to any body or head covering, and the term *burqa* is the most consistently used term for any Muslim head and body coverings by both Muslims and non-Muslims.

Veiling is not a recent phenomenon but an ancient cultural practice that antedates the Islamic Republic of Iran by thousands of years and predates the culture of Arabia even before the lifetime of Muhammad. The first known reference to veiling was made in an Assyrian legal text of the thirteenth century BCE, which decreed that veiling was a 'sign of nobility' reserved only for 'respectable women'; that is, it was prohibited for prostitutes to wear a veil. Harlots or slave girls improperly wearing a veil in public were punished (Shirazi 2000:114). In recent times, it has given rise to endless debate, discussion and interpretation. It is evident that, as elsewhere in the world, religion is only one element that is involved when discussing dress.

Popular media representations of Muslim women swathed in black often give the impression that Islamic dress is about sombre uniformity and conformity, but as Emma Tarlo points out with reference to Muslims in Britain, a stroll down any multicultural British high street creates a very different impression. In Britain, young fashionable Muslim girls can be seen wearing the latest jeans, jackets, dresses, skirts and tops and the only identifiable Muslim dress feature is some form of headscarf, fashionably coordinated with the rest of their outfit which in recent years has become a 'new form of personal art', contrasting strongly with the austere full-length 'billowing *burqa*' worn by some Muslim women (Tarlo 2010:1).

Burqas elsewhere are styled according to the percentage of the body covered, the specific parts of the body hidden from view, and the interpretation as to what female modesty entails. A woman of the Boyevahmad tribe in Iran might cover her head in delicate gauze veiling finely decorated with metallic floral shapes and coin fringing but leave her face bare. At the other extreme is the stark plain black heavy full-face *burqa* that covers the entire body from top to toe with only a grill through which to peek. Between these two extremes is a variety of intriguing combinations of 'seeing' and 'not seeing' the woman's face, neck and head.

A Bedouin tribeswoman of Dubai might wear a silver-sprinkled gauze head cover with a stiffened satin beak-line *milfa*, or face mask, whereas a Bedouin woman of Oman might dress in a full-face black mask, the entire face being covered by a kind of cloth or leather mask with a stiffened extension that runs vertically on the top of the mask from hairline to beyond the chin, held in place by an *asayib*, or circlet of cloth, with only two small holes for the eyes, giving the impression of a medieval warrior. Equally concealing from prying male eyes, or even the occasional sideways glance, is the ornate brightly coloured red and yellow head covering and silver coin-trimmed mask of the Harb Bedouin women of Saudi Arabia.

The term *hijab* literally means 'curtain' and stems from the Arabic *hajaba*, meaning 'to veil, cover, screen, shelter, seclude (from); to hide, obscure (from sight); to eclipse, outshine, overshadow; to make imperceptible, invisible; to conceal (from); to make or form a separation (between)' (Shirazi 2000:115). Thus, it can be understood in many different ways. It is also spelt *hejab/hijaab* and when used in a religious context refers to the concept of covering practices of both Muslim men and women under Islam. One dresses in a 'hijaab-like manner' (Daly 2000:137), that is, loose-fitting garments that do not hug the body. Wearing the *hijab* has become an identity issue with many Muslim women in places where choice is possible. Some women wear veils, some do not. Some wear a simple scarf over their heads, while some cultures insist on the most concealing of all, the *chador* (Persian for 'tent'), which is head-to-toe veiling, with only a latticed opening for the eyes.

To wear or not to wear the veil has become a political as well as an identity issue for Muslims. In either its simple or extreme form, the veil epitomizes the faith of Muslims and often demonstrates the rejection of Western influences.

Iran

Faegheh Shirazi, who originates from Iran, writes that it is compulsory for all women to wear the veil in the country—even foreign women. Every time she visited her home country, she says, she 'chafed at the necessity of wearing this cumbersome attire', but 'always complied with the dress code in order to avoid being harassed or imprisoned' (Shirazi 2000:113).

Women's dress is full of all kinds of implicit meanings made visibly explicit. It can, at the same time, symbolically and silently convey her degree of religiosity, her affiliation with, or protest against, a political party, her strong belief in the feminist movement or her allegiance with the struggle against colonial regimes. However, it might be simply a means of protecting herself from being hassled outside her home.

The *chador* was worn by religious women in Iran as proper attire for praying, visiting holy sites and entering mosques and shrines. This particular style of veil is an outerwear floor-length piece of fabric (body and headwrap), cut in semicircular shape, placed on the head and covering the head and the entire body. The *chador* requires experience and practice in order to be worn properly and gracefully, since it does not have any fastening devices, sleeves or a place for the neck to be slipped into. When the *chador* is worn, a woman must make sure that it is securely placed on her head, properly draped, with its corners levelled at both ends. Perhaps the most difficult part of handling this veil is that at all times one hand of its wearer is occupied holding it in place, which means that all other activities need to be done with one hand, making both shopping and carrying a baby extremely taxing.

The *maghnae*, a head covering that was adopted in Iran in combination with the *chador*, possibly from a neighbouring Arab nation (Shirazi 2000:120), is a semicircular sewn garment that tightly covers the head and loosely covers the chest and shoulder areas, resembling the habit of Catholic nuns. The *maghnae* has a fastening device, such as snaps or ties, and frames the face to ensure that the hair is always covered. The preferred colour of the whole orthodox ensemble is black or navy blue, both colours that are uncomfortable to wear in hot climates.

The less orthodox style of veiling commonly used in Iran consists of a head cover called *rusari* ('placed upon the head'), and an outer gown, or *rupush* ('worn outside' or 'worn over garments'). The *rusari* is a large, square scarf that can be stylishly and loosely draped over the head. It can be made fashionable using different designs, colours, fabrics, and embellished by adding coins, beads, embroidery, fringes, tassels, pins and pieces of jewellery.

The same applies to *rupush*, the outerwear gown that is used along with the headscarf, which can be individualized with the addition of pockets, gathers, slits and embellishments, according to whatever is fashionable. However, any departure from the orthodox style raises all sorts of debates and clashes with what Shirazi terms the 'chastity patrols', or 'moral police' (Shirazi 2000:120).

While veiling has always existed in Iranian culture, it has been imposed and revived by the present government in Iran, and two distinct versions of the *hijab* have developed: the orthodox, more severe form of black veiling, derived from the traditional form of Iranian *chador* with an additional headpiece, and a second style of *hijab*, which is a looser, more Western style of veiling. This latter form has resulted in accusations of 'improper veiling' in Iran and some other Islamic cultures. A fashionable modern hijab or a dab of lipstick can land a woman in jail.

At the time of Shirazi's (2000) publication, the government of Iran was actively implementing the *hijab* and the code of ethics among its populace. Muslim women's honour and chastity were ostensibly being protected by emphasizing religious morality. The law, writes Shirazi (2000:117), filtered down to public areas in Iran, with shop signs informing female customers that service would be denied to women in 'improper *hijab*'.

Men and women have both tried to make sense out of a large body of religious writings dealing with issues of clothing in religious contexts such as the Qur'an, the *hadith*, as well as the Shar'ia (Islamic law based on the Qur'anic and hadith interpretation). El Guindi (1999:140) identifies four themes: (1) bodily modesty, (2) averting distraction in worship, (3) moderation in daily life, and (4) distinguishing Muslim identity through aversion of certain forms of dress such as colour. With reference to the latter, in order not to cause distraction during worship, the Prophet Muhammad asked that the *khamisa*, dress that was made out of fabric of silk or wool, striped and with a decorative design, be replaced with an *anbaganiyya*, dress in an opaque heavy material with no embroidery or decorative designs. Men were also advised to avoid wearing gold, large rings, silk fabric clothes or colourful fabric to emphasize moderation and to highlight their distinctively Islamic identity.

Women are addressed in the Qur'an on more than one occasion; the particular verses dealing with veiling are in the chapter *Nur* (24:30–31) of the Qur'an:

The believing men are enjoined to lower their gaze and conceal their genitals [30] and the believing women are enjoined to lower their gaze and conceal their genitals, draw their *khimar* [headveil] to cover their cleavage [breasts], and not display their beauty except that which has to be revealed, except to their husbands, their fathers, their husbands' fathers, their sons, their husbands' sons, their brothers or their brothers' sons, or their sister's sons, or their women, or the slaves, or eunuchs or children under age; and they should not strike their feet to draw attention to their hidden beauty. O believers turn to God, that you may attain bliss.

Whether such veiling necessitates *hijab* or *chador* is therefore unclear. Faegheh Shirazi points out that in the Preamble of the 1979 Islamic Republic Constitution, it was emphasized that one of the main issues of government concern was the protection of a woman's sexuality; however, this is open to various interpretations with regard to the extent of body coverage. A woman was expected to wear *hijab*, but it does not necessarily mean that her *hijab* should be a *chadur* (*chador*) (Shirazi 2000:117). Later *fatwa* (Islamic legal opinion) narrowed this interpretation down by insisting that the 'best and most superior form of *hijab* is *chadur*' (Shirazi 2000:125).

The more orthodox, conservative groups chose the 'superior' form of dress and the *hijab* began to be viewed as a more modern Western adaptation of women's dress. Cultural and political Islamic sentiments can take precedence over religious interpretations of sacred texts. Merely being covered is not enough.

Afghanistan

In Afghanistan, total dress coverage of a woman's body is called *chadri*, described by Louis Dupree (1980:246) as 'a sack-like garment of pleated colored silk or rayon, [which] covers the entire body from head to toe, with an embroidered lattice-work eye-mask to permit limited vision'. It is worn on top of other clothing such as a dress or *payraahan*, a pant or *tumbaan*, and head covering, or *chaadar*.

The *chaadaree* is further distinguished by the *chishim* band, a rectangular area of drawn-work hand embroidery that covers the eye and provides limited vision for the wearer as well as minimal view of the wearer by an observer. The *chaadaree* is a seamed and pleated garment that is vertically panelled and made from approximately seven yards or metres of cotton or silk fabric or synthetic equivalents. It is composed of three separate units: the hat, or *kulla*; the face, or *rooy* band, with a region referred to as the eye or *chisim* band; and pleated fabric, or *teka* (Daly 2000:134). The total garment is considered the most respectable outfit for a woman to wear outside the home. Underneath this tent-like fabric structure, however, might be hidden luxurious undergarments, and decorative jewellery.

The *chaadaree* is utilitarian, providing warmth in very cold weather while still protecting the wearer from harsh heat, sun and humidity. The most

Figure 3.4 *Burqa*-clad Afghan Muslim women. Photo: Getty Images.

practical aspect, however, is to protect women from the unwanted male gaze. Depending upon the fabric from which it is made, the *chaadaree* can visibly display Afghani class status by the colour, cleanliness and quality of its fabric, the number and fineness of the pleats, and the hand embroidery on it. Most women have only one *chaadaree*, replacing worn areas with new fabrics and re-pleating and re-dyeing when needed.

One Afghan woman remarked about wearing the *chaadaree*:

Some veils were chic and stylish, with special shorter cap designs. Veils also differed in the fineness of the eye mesh, the quality of the material and the way the numerous pleats were set, narrow pleats being considered more stylish than wide ones.

Wearing the veil for the first time was very difficult for me but I came to find that it was not so bad. . . . Concealing your identity behind a veil and watching the world through a four-by-six-inch rectangle of fine mesh had certain advantages. It was a sign of respect, of growing up and womanhood. (cited in Daly 2000:141)

Partial covering is more commonly worn throughout Afghanistan and is referred to as *chaadar*. Made of two to three yards of fabric, the *chaadar* is the most common form of covering worn by women on a daily basis. Typically, it covers the head, including the hair, neck and shoulders of the wearer and is more analogous to the Western notion of a scarf or shawl. It is considered a 'partial veil' and is worn as part of an ensemble of clothing. The type of fabric selected depends on a number of things, one of which is climate. During cool weather a lightweight wool challis head covering might be worn, while a heavier-weight wool *chaadar* might be selected for wear during the winter months.

In Afghanistan, fabrics are handwoven from cotton or wool, or made of fine silk, the texture of the fabric important because it adds to the soft draped affect and flows with bodily movements, most likely an important point when all signs of visibility are absent. Some women like the luxurious feel of silk, as well as the prestige of wearing a more costly fabric. One Afghan woman said: 'I can close my eyes and feel by the touch of my hand, a finely woven silk crepe' (Daly 1999:154). Crêpe gives a soft appearance as well as being soft to touch.

During holy pilgrimage to Mecca, a white head covering is worn by Afghani women. White *chaadar* are also worn weekly on Friday, *Juma*, the holy day when Muslims attend mosque. Maintaining the cleanliness of a white *chaadar* is more labour intensive and necessitates more use of scarce water resources than *chaadars* of other colours (Daly 2000:137). Older Afghani women tend to wear muted and darker *chaadar* than younger women who prefer more lively colours frequently in floral patterns, embroidered with gold or vibrant embroidered greens with velvet dresses and satin pants. Once a young girl enters puberty and starts menstruating she wears a *chaadar* as a marker of her change to adult female status and being of a marriageable age (Daly 1999:155).

For some Muslim women in Western cultures, looking Muslim is a subtle process, involving the layering of fashionable garments so as not to reveal too much flesh or body shape. For others, it may involve choosing to wear a T-shirt, a very Western item, but with '100% Muslim' printed on it, or wearing full-length traditional clothing but made from tracksuit material.

Some garments might be imported from the Middle East or purchased over the Internet from, among others, the popular online store www.thehijabshop.

com. The first Muslim lifestyle magazine to be produced in Britain, *Emel*, launched in 2003, shows very modern, colourful, cosmopolitan Muslims and includes features on fashion, cooking, gardening and informative articles that include a variety of opinions about all topics, including dress options, with attempts being made to develop new visibly Muslim men's fashions adapted to a Western environment (Tarlo 2010).

In some cultures, there have been some innovative and imaginative ways of 'covering up' while still having freedom of movement and fitting in with another cultural lifestyle. Nowhere is this more evident than in twenty-first-century Australia.

The *Burqini*

The edict for women to be fully covered has had some repercussions in countries like Australia, with its predominant mode of leisure revolving around water sports and beach culture. As the majority of the population of Australia lives on the extensive coastline of this continent, the beach is home for many, and beach dress consists mainly of various ways in which to uncover the body without being completely nude.

Young Muslims living in Australia who want to adhere to Muslim dress codes, yet participate in beach culture and water sports, are faced with a dilemma: the Australian choice of minimal coverage or adhering to the Islamic code of covering the body in order to maintain Islamic allegiance. This dilemma has been creatively resolved by the introduction of a unique mode of dress: the *burqini*, which offers an acceptable compromise to all concerned (Hume 2010:192).

The *burqini* (a conflation of *burqa* and bikini) is a top-to-toe two-piece Lycra swimsuit with *hijab* attached, designed by Lebanese Australian Aheda Zanetti with the intention of satisfying even the strictest of dress codes with regard to bodily coverage and modesty but which is comfortable and light enough to enable swimming. The head, neck and arms are completely covered by a thigh-length, long-sleeve dress, which is worn over loose pants with straight legs. The only parts of the body revealed are the face, hands and feet.

This swimsuit is available in different colours, is chlorine resistant with low water absorbency and is very quick to dry. Printed motifs over the chest area provide extra modesty to that area of the body. Because of the Australian government health advice to 'slip, slop, slap' all exposed areas with suntan lotion, hats, and cover-ups while in the extreme heat of the midday sun, many Australians cover their children, and even themselves, with Lycra cover-ups to

Figure 3.5   *Burqini*-clad lifeguard in Sydney, Australia. Photo: Getty Images.

avoid skin cancer that is highly prevalent in this sun-loving country. The *burqini* is not dissimilar to the new trend of Lycra cover-ups.

Burqini-garbed women have even joined Surf Life Saving teams, whose bronzed, blonde-haired men and women are as quintessentially an Australian icon as the ANZAC digger with his slouched hat. The *burqini* reflects Islamic mores with regard to acceptable Islamic dress in a way that demonstrates the adaptability and innovativeness of a religion that has found its way to a country which has quite different attitudes and beliefs about the clothed and unclothed body, both secular and sacred.

PART II

EASTERN RELIGIONS

−4−

India: Hindus, Holy Sadhus, Sikhs and Jains

This chapter explores the vast range of beliefs within India, the sounds and smells of India and the extraordinary colours and textures that pervade the country's various religions. India's major religion, Hinduism, has a pantheon of gods and goddesses whose symbols reflect various functions and manifestations of the one supreme and eternal Divine Absolute. The individual gods Brahma, Vishnu and Shiva are manifestations of the One, but they are only three among thousands.

The population of India reached 844 million people in the 1990s, 83 per cent of whom are Hindu (Kennett 1994:140). Hindus, Muslims, Christians, Sikhs and Buddhists all coexist throughout India, as well as smaller offshoots of Hinduism, specific groups such as the Hare Krishna, and vestiges of tribal religions in northern India. There are also individual holy mendicants, such as the *sadhus*, as well as those who practice extreme forms of bodily privations and austerities. India is a rich and colourful country for religious diversity, religious dress and body decoration. Where orthodox religion plays a greater role, dress codes are strict. This chapter will cover, specifically, the clothing pertaining to Hindus, Jains, Sikhs and peripatetic holy men such as the *sadhus*.

There are a multitude of ways throughout India to express beliefs through dress and adornment, the most basic principle being that one dresses according to one's caste, gender, social status and age group. Clothing fabrics vary from exquisite gold brocades, shimmering silks, and jewelled, beaded and mirrored cottons to basic plain, monochromatic cottons. In India, dress extends from humans to animals, especially elephants, as well as temples, altars and vehicles; even statues of deities are daily bathed, dressed and adorned with elaborate care. Colours and textures mingle with the sounds of jangling gold, silver and glass bangles, anklets with bells, long earrings, toe rings, nose rings, and necklaces. Incense from temples, those quiet refuges from the noisy world outside, float out into the hustle and bustle of crowded streets with their smells of food, marigolds, cow manure, urine and body odours, all of which tend to seep into the fabrics of wearers' clothes.[1]

Men's dress in India can be roughly distinguished in the major religions as the white *kurta*-pyjama, vest, cap, and beard of the Muslim; the white *dhoti-kurta*, topknot, bare feet and clean shaven face of the Hindu; the colourful baggy *jurta*-pyjama, turban, curly shoes, and full beard and moustache of the Sikh; the stitched grey suit of pants, jacket and hat of the Parsi; and the Christian man in Western-style dark suit with no particular haircut or facial hair, who is generally hatless (Shukla 2008:45). Among Hindus, there is no special dress for religious festivals or other festivities; however, on occasions such as these, all who can afford it put on richer and better clothes than those ordinarily worn.

Turbans once defined a man's caste, class and region all over India, but now most men go bareheaded, except in Rajasthan, where a turban's colour and folding indicates class, caste or trade, and among the Sikhs, whose main region is in the Punjab, north of Rajasthan, and who wind up their long hair beneath their turban.

THE SARI

The most ubiquitous dress for women throughout all of India is the sari,[2] which evolved its system of folds and drapes over a long time. Its accompanying garments—petticoats, blouses (*coli/choli*) and underwear—were introduced by British missionaries. All over India, shops sell an enormous variety of saris, made of silk, cotton, georgette, organza, chiffon, crêpe, and taffeta, as well as synthetic materials such as nylon, acrylic and polyester (Shukla 2008), all in an amazing splash of colour and textures, such as block prints on silk and tie-dyed cotton saris, and often shimmering or catching the eye through additional embellishments such as sequins, beads and mirrors.

The most common type of sari worn today in India is a mass-produced synthetic one which came about with the introduction of textile mills and power looms. With five metres of fabric to be wrapped, pleated, tucked and draped, with no or very few safety pins or other devices to hold it in place, the sari requires expertise and much practice for it to be worn with elegance and aplomb.

Attention has to be given to the folding of one of the five metres of cloth into pleats that are tucked in at the waist to fall softly over the lower half of the body, and to the positioning of the drape across the breasts and over one shoulder, with the *pallu*, or free end of the sari, falling gracefully down the back. The whole cloth usually has a border on either side which gives the *pallu*, the decorative end piece of the sari, and the hem a contrasting and defining look, the colours often picked up in the blouse. An additional strip of cloth can be sewn on to the inside of the hem to give weight and strength to the border.

Underneath the sari a petticoat is worn, which is a simple long skirt tied with a drawstring, usually not visible unless the woman is doing chores. The blouse is close fitting and short, leaving a bare midriff, with sleeves reaching almost to the elbow. The whole ensemble, with the addition of *bindi*, earrings, necklaces, bangles and sandals, creates a vision of statuesque feminine elegance. While the total lower half of the body is hidden, the upper half reveals the arms, midriff and the neck and face. To wear a sari is a sensual experience, as Banerjee and Miller (2003:25) write:

> The two shoulders and the two breasts are touched by the garment in quite different ways. The right shoulder can remain untouched by the sari, while the left bears the weight of the *pallu*. The right breast feels the pressure of the pleats of the *pallu* pulled across the bosom, whereas the left one feels strangely exposed, covered from the front but visible from the side. The right side of the waist is hot from the pleats passing over it, but the left side is uncovered and cool.

As well, various fabrics create different sensations on the skin. A soft silk or chiffon feels different than a cotton sari that has been starched with homemade rice or a sari with a prickly gold border that scratches the skin. The woman's movements and the way she walks in a sari are determined by the five metres of fabric remaining in their proper place; the length of the stride is kept in check, and one arm is constantly ensuring that the *pallu* remains over the shoulder or in its position of covering the breast, and the pleats have to remain in place. As the actress Deena Pathak expressed:

> Other clothing is on you, but it is not with you. But the sari is with me. I have to constantly handle it. I just can't let it lie. The whole thing creates movement and one is moving with it all the time. That is why the *pallu* is not stitched. And that is the grace of the sari. (Banerjee and Miller 2003:23)

A woman's sari is intimately linked to its wearer. One old woman commented:

> Now I have a fever and don't feel good so I don't feel like wearing my new sari [. . .] This old one feels much better as it is soft and old, and it's light. In general it is better to wear old saris when doing housework since it is soft and you know where it is. A new one is crisp and you can't control it and tie it around your waist, and then it might catch fire in front of the hearth. (Banerjee and Miller 2003:28)

Figure 4.1   Old woman in sari, India. Photo: Dianne Osborne.

The sari is dynamic, versatile, and constantly moving and is an integral part of the wearer's life. It is truly a living item of apparel that has numerous functional and practical uses. The *pallu* in particular has a multitude of uses: wiping away sweat, cleaning a child's face, helping to lift hot vessels in the kitchen, cleaning spectacles, protecting the head and face from the hot sun, filtering out smoke or smog by covering the face or for wiping a table.

One Indian woman living in America reminisced about the rustle and smell of the sari:

A silk sari has a smell when you open it, and when I open my own saris and get that smell I get very excited. It makes you homesick. That smell stays when you walk and you pull the *pallu* and you get that smell. There is the fragrance of jasmine, rose, and henna.

When I imagine a sari, I always imagine nice silk saris. With a beautiful color and border . . . a combination of border, material, color, and the designs. I don't know, when we put on the saris and the jewelry, it's like a romantic mode, yeah you are in honeymoon. When you wear a very nice sari and you dress up and that whole thing, your mind is very different, like you are in a dream world when you put it on. (Littrell and Ogle 2007:124)

Another woman remembered the smell surrounding the ritual nature of caring for her hair which added to the overall impression of the sari's elegance:

When I was a girl, my mother would put oil in my hair and wash it and braid it and put flowers in it . . . Sundays, everybody puts oil in their hair, waits for one or two hours and goes for shampooing. It was a ritual kind of thing—almost a ceremony. Everybody, my sisters too, would put oil and then one by one you would go to the bathroom and your mom or somebody would help you shampoo. Once you got into the bathroom the whole body would be massaged with oil. When you came out the skin would feel soft, the hair would feel soft. (Littrell and Ogle 2007:124)

Indian women generally have thick, long, shiny, healthy and beautiful hair. Babies' heads are more often than not shaved on their first birthday so that their first hair can be given as a gift to God, and their heads are massaged with sandalwood to encourage thick regrowth. Girls are often seen massaging oil into each other's scalps. Body hair however is regarded as very unattractive and is either plucked or shaved.

Some women's 'religious sensibility' dictates their wearing a sari according to days of the week and their association with certain deities; for example white on Monday for Siva, red on Tuesday for Mahavir. Colours thus worn make a sari 'auspicious' (Banerjee and Miller 2003:51). However, a woman is more likely to select materials and colours that suit her complexion. The sari becomes a rite of passage for girls who don one for the first time, and a woman might be presented with a sari on the birth of her first child. The iconic sari of motherhood in Bengal is white with a red border.

Regional Variations of Sari

There are geographic variations in the way a sari is draped, wrapped and tucked. In some places, women of a particular subcaste are distinguished by their sari style; in a village in Madhya Pradesh for example, women of one subcaste wear only printed saris, a variety that is forbidden to another subcaste (Banerjee and Miller 2003). There is a profound distinction between pure and impure in Hindu cosmology, and the fear of pollution is strong. Bodily fluids such as saliva, semen or blood are considered highly polluting, and anyone with an occupation that necessarily involves direct contact with any of these substances is ranked at the bottom of India's hierarchy. While in the West secondhand clothing is acceptable to wear, and even sought after by the budget-conscious or those looking for something different, secondhand clothing in India is looked upon with great suspicion, as it is associated both with the fear of pollution and extreme poverty. As well, given the numerous functional uses of the sari, such as wiping off sweat, a secondhand sari is not seen as an option for the majority of Indians.

The saris and scarves of the Rajasthani women in the northern provinces of India are particularly vivid, contrasting with the arid sandy landscape. The saris, both decorative and practical, are intricately woven or embroidered and are the subject of many Rajput love songs. When the sun becomes too strong, the long scarf can be pulled down and used as a sun visor or wrapped around the body if the weather becomes a little cooler. Rajasthani women also wear masses of jingling, shining jewellery: bracelets that almost cover their arms, glittering ring noses and anklets that make sounds as they walk.

TEXTILES AND JEWELLERY

A visit to a textile shop in India is like entering Aladdin's magic cave; the colours and fabrics are incredible, and when a customer arrives in a shop, one or two male sellers can end up sitting behind a pile of exquisite layers of fabric that reaches to their chests. The party of a bride-to-be might spend several hours in the one shop as the shopkeeper throws swaths of colours and textiles one on top of the other to encourage the bridal party to select something for the entire bridal party.[3]

In the ancient world, cotton, wool and silk cloth from Benares (Varanasi) called *kasikuttam, kaseyka* or simply *kasiya*, was famous the world over for its fine texture and softness. Banaras is famous for its silk brocade. The cloth in which Buddha's body was wrapped after his death came from Banaras and was said to have been woven so fine that it could not absorb even oil. The heritage of excellence of Banarasi fabrics is evident in the saris, whose distinguishing feature is its *zari* work—gold and silver threads woven into patterns. In earlier days, the threads were made of real gold and silver, making them prized possessions. Now, synthetic gold threads have taken their place.

Jewellery such as earrings, bracelets, necklaces and ankle bracelets are worn, and noses may be pierced and a stud-type jewel or a nose ring added. As well as their visual éclat, some items of jewellery, particularly bangles and anklets, are remarkable for their sounds:

If you're wearing bangles . . . they make certain sounds. So, I always like the glass bangles, the more traditional. They break very easily, so I started buying metal ones, but they don't make the sound like a glass bangle. I always like to wear long earrings. It [all] has to move. You can feel something moving. Something that enhances the contours . . . The bangles showing your wrist, a little bit, even if you have a small bracelet. The anklets, I loved when I got married. And that lets you know that there is a new bride in the house. (Littrell and Ogle 2007:123)

Women wear their hair parted in the centre and usually braided. If they are married, they smear red make-up into the parting of their hair. Women may wear a *tika* (a dot of turmeric powder or other coloured substance) on their foreheads as a symbol of their religion. On a man, it is referred to as a *tilak*.

Tika is usually made from red vermillion paste, white sandalwood paste or ash and can be used to denote religious sects, roughly divided into two main groups: three horizontal bars indicate the person is a Shaivige (follower of Shiva), whereas vertical stripes indicate a Vaishnavige (follower of Vishnu). The central stroke on a Vaishnavige's forehead is usually red, representing the radiance of the goddess Lakshmi, the wife of Vishnu in his incarnation as Natayan. The small dot which women and girls place on their foreheads is known as a *bindi*. These are usually bought ready-made from the market and have become a fashion accessory, with every imaginable shape and colour to match the occasion.

HINDUS

Hindus[4] are born into a complex caste system which consists of four main groups: Brahmins (priests and theologians), Kshatriyas (warriors and rulers), Vaisyas (merchants, traders and farmers) and Sudras (craftsmen and workers). These are subdivided into myriad hierarchical *jati*, or groups of 'families'. Beneath the four main castes are the Dalits, formerly known as Untouchables. Hinduism contains no single doctrine, nor does it have a single founder or teacher.

The principal concepts of Hinduism are reincarnation, the caste system, merging with ultimate reality, living a moral life and attaining *moksha*, the escape from the cycle of continuing reincarnations. Hinduism contains pantheons of gods and goddesses, which are fundamentally symbols that depict various attributes, functions and manifestations of the one supreme and eternal Divine Absolute, the cause and foundation of all existence. Hindus acknowledge many deities but usually devote their prayers and practices to one or a few, and this may depend upon context.

Hinduism does not impose rigid beliefs and practices on any of its more than 800 million followers; instead, each person follows a path to self-realization in a number of ways: worship, chanting, devotional surrender, service, yoga, meditation and self-knowledge. Rituals and Hindu philosophy draw upon a large collection of philosophical literature and scriptures that include the Vedas, the Upanishads, the Brahma Sutras, the Bhagavad-Gita and the epics Ramayana and the Mahabharatha. Traces of Hinduism go back around three thousand years, yet while beliefs and practices vary widely across the continent, there are some commonalities among which are the notions of re-incarnation (*samsara*), conduct or action (*karma*), appropriate behaviour for one's station in life (*dharma*) and the pervasive caste system.

There are festivals and ceremonies associated not only with gods and goddesses but also with the sun, moon, planets, rivers, oceans, trees and animals, and the streets of India are continuously full of people, sounds, smells and a riot of vivid colours. Dress widens its parameters in India, extending from humans to clothed, painted and jewel-bedecked animals, especially elephants, as well as to the brightly painted statues of deities to be found within glittering ornate temples, where the sounds of chiming temple bells are often heard, converging with the smell of incense, golden marigold blossoms and hot bodies. Ochre red is a favourite colour for smearing idols and deities in all parts of India.

Seeing and Being Seen

Visually attractive dress is important not only for presenting a beautiful body to human onlookers, but also to nonhuman onlookers. Divine spirits called *Murtas* are said to reside in stone, wood or metal images called *murtis*, receptacles into which a deity can be embodied. The concept of *darshan* (Sanskrit) means seeing and being seen by the gods; it is the two-way gaze between devotee and deity, the moment of communication with a god during the act of *puja* (worship). Therefore, to go into a temple improperly attired might displease the gods and shows disrespect. The clothing, jewellery and sweet, clean smell of the devotee are all mirrored in the offerings that are given to the *murtis*, who are equally bestowed with flowers, rings, bangles, bindis, hair ribbons and small amounts of food and sweets to please them. In the winter, they are suitably clothed to keep them warm, and at certain times of the year, they are dressed in new clothes (Eck 1998; Shukla 2008).

The section of the body considered to be the focus of a woman's beauty is the eyes, and the naturally large dark eyes of Indian women are greatly enhanced with black kohl. Even babies are regularly decorated with black kohl around their eyes. Many infants are adorned with amulets tied with thread around various parts of the body, namely the neck, waist and wrist, to ward off malevolent spirits and to deflect the evil eye of jealous humans.

A Hindu wedding is a lavish and colourful ceremony that is the occasion of the most dazzling display of dress that one could find anywhere in the world, with exquisite gold-brocaded saris, shimmering silks and fabrics heavy with sumptuous jewels, beads or sequins. A bride wears a colourful *sari*, often red and gold (symbolizing happiness), and her hands are decorated with intricate lace-like henna patterns. She wears an extensive array of jewellery, ranging from layers of bangles, nose rings, earrings, gold necklaces, anklets, toe rings, *bindi* (between the eyes) and heavy make-up. The bridegroom traditionally wears a white or brocaded outfit, topped with a colourful turban. During the ceremony, the bride and groom exchange garlands of flowers which they wear around their necks.

Figure 4.2 Henna hands and bangles, India. Photo: Dianne Osborne.

Henna and *Mehndi*

Henna is used extensively as a form of body adornment known as *mehndi* and has been practiced for thousands of years throughout India, Africa and the Middle East (Fabius 1998; Batra 1999). The paste that is applied to the body is made from the crushed leaves of the henna plant (*Lawsonia inermis*). Fresh henna leaves have no odour, even when crushed between the fingers, but powdered henna has an earthy, clay-like smell. The tiny delicate flower has four petals, with a long slender stamen at the centre. When it blooms, it emits a sweet fragrance like jasmine and rose. For centuries, perfumers have made much use of the scents that can be made from the flower's oil.

When applied to the skin, the colour produced by the henna plant is a variation of reddish brown. Depending on the skin tone, skin type, body temperature and other factors, the colour might appear as any one of the following: light orange, dark orange, reddish brown, cafe-au-lait brown, tobacco brown, chocolate brown or burgundy, and sometimes even crimson red. Body designs using henna paste vary according to culture and religious beliefs.

In India, henna is used extensively during a woman's preparation for her marriage. It is thought very auspicious if the henna stain remains on the body for some time after marriage, as it indicates that the mother-in-law of the bride will look favourably upon her. The deeper the colour stains into the skin, the longer the love between the couple is supposed to last. Hence, a good *mehndi* application is almost a prayer to the gods for everlasting love and a successful marriage. Designs vary; some are applied so finely and intricately that they give the appearance of delicate lace. A yellow turmeric paste, *haldi*, is often applied to the groom's body, and he might wear a red dye *tika* on his forehead. In India, a custom is to hide the initials of the new husband within an intricate henna design on the hands and feet of the new bride. After marriage, bright red in the parting of a woman's hair indicates that she is a married woman (Batra 1999).

In the south and eastern territories of India, in places such as Pondicherry, Chennai (Madras) and Calcutta, henna is not available, and people are not familiar with *mehndi* practice. Instead, eastern Indians use a reddish ink called *alta* for decorative purposes, and they paint only bold simple designs. Southerners use the bark of sandalwood trees to make a yellowish-brown paste, which is also used for decorative painting of *tilaks* or *bindis* between the eyes for prayer purposes.

Hindus and Death

The three main practices of death rituals in India are cremation (the archetypical practice for death among Hindus throughout India), burial and 'outside disintegration', also referred to as sky burial, as the body is left outside for circling vultures to strip the flesh off the bones. Hindus view cremation as most spiritually beneficial to the departed soul because, as the astral body tends to have a lingering attachment to the corpse, burning the body within twenty-four hours of death enables the soul to begin its onward journey as soon as possible (Kramer 1988).

At the onset of death, the eldest son and other relatives put water into the dying person's mouth, preferably water that has been taken from the sacred Ganges River. When the person is declared dead, the body is washed and anointed, the hair and beard (if male) are trimmed, the thumbs are tied together, as are the big toes, and the body is dressed in new white cotton clothes. If the deceased is a woman who has died before her husband, she may be wrapped in red cloth, indicating her married status and the auspicious state of having died before becoming widowed (Hertel 2009). A lamp is kept burning throughout the mourning period. The chief mourner, usually the eldest son, has his head shaved to show that he is in mourning, and leads the way to the cremation site, carrying a clay pot filled with burning incense, and is followed by mourners bearing a bamboo stretcher containing the corpse.

Death is not hidden in India, and any tourist to India may see a corpse being borne on bamboo stretchers decorated with flowers through the streets and alleyways to the ceremonial funeral pyre. This is especially likely in the holy city of Varanasi, a popular tourist destination, where it is almost impossible not to see cremations at any one of several *ghats* along the river. Upon reaching its destination at one of the *ghats*, the body is burnt on a pyre in full public view. To die in Varanasi is to be liberated; even people who die and are cremated elsewhere try to arrange for their ashes to be sent to Varanasi for immersion in the waters of the holy Ganges.

Upon returning home, mourners take a purification bath, and an oil lamp is lit in the place where the body had been lying, to light the way of the deceased's soul. During the following day or days, mourners return to the cremation site to collect the ashes which are then deposited in a river, ideally the Ganges, to await reincarnation. During the days of impurity following a death, food restrictions are adhered to, and house cleaning is abandoned. Men of the household stop shaving and cutting their hair, and all family members refrain from cutting their fingernails and toenails for a period of ten days, after which they all undergo water purification by bathing, and the house is thoroughly cleaned (Hertel 2009).

In earlier times, a widow would be expected to mount the funeral pyre of her deceased husband, burning in the flames with him while she is still alive. The term *suttee* (*sati*) describes both the ritual and the woman herself. The *sati* at the funeral was often dressed in her marriage robes or other finery. Bangles symbolize the married state, and the ritual moment when a wife breaks her bangles signals her entry into the inauspicious state of widowhood. These bangles remain unbroken on the woman performing *sati*, indicating that she continues her wifely status, denying separation from her husband even at death (Hawley 1994).

Symbolic of the act of *sati*, a simple hand held up with palm facing the viewer and with intact, unbroken bangles, is depicted on stones and shrines throughout Rajasthan and other parts of northern India. Shrines to the *sati* are decorated and venerated annually by her descendants, and the *sati* herself is regarded as a goddess, having performed the ultimate service of loyalty and self-sacrifice for her husband. When a woman performs *sati*, she becomes a *satimata*, literally 'sati mother', and is regarded as a local deity who primarily protects members of her family lineages. The *chunari*, a rite that solemnizes the death of a *sati*, takes place twelve days after her death. *Chunari* is so named because of the long piece of cloth that is placed on the ashes of the *sati* in the course of its celebration.

While *sati* has always been the exception rather than the rule in Hindu life and is now illegal, it nevertheless occurred even as late as 1987, when a nineteen-year-old widow, Roop Kanwar, dressed in her red wedding dress, died on the burning funeral pyre of her deceased husband in Rajasthan (Hawley 1994).

Extreme pain appears to form a sacrificial role in India in other ways, as will be seen in the Hindu festival of Thaipusam, practiced in some parts of India, and exported to places such as Singapore, where a two-day Hindu festival is held annually.

Thaipusam and the *Kavadi* Burden

Thaipusam[5] is a Hindu festival where men, women and boys practice self-mortification and austerities as they fulfil their vows to Hindu deities. The festival is held in honour of Lord Subramaniam, a son of Lord Shiva, in his aspect as Lord Murugan. Subramaniam is one of the major gods in the Hindu pantheon and is considered the personification of youth, virtue, bravery and power. What began as a simple festival to celebrate the triumph of good over evil has become a visual and startling display of physical mortification, with devotees fulfilling their vows to Lord Murugan. The reasons for undertaking the ordeal are varied: to thank Lord Murugan for having overcome an illness, for a woman having found a husband or having become pregnant, for having helped in difficult exams or for good fortune and a better life.

To prepare for the rigours of Thaipusam, devotees purify their bodies and their minds by refraining from alcohol, cigarettes, sexual intercourse and any contamination, such as contact with a menstruating woman, for forty-eight hours prior to the festival. They eat only a vegetarian diet, sleep on the floor and do not shave or cut their hair. They must not use any utensils which others have touched. There must have been no recent deaths in the family; otherwise, the pollution of death will cling to them. Thaipusam is a visible display of religious agony and ecstasy and a demonstration of love, devotion and gratitude to the deity.

The most outstanding item of dress worn by devotees during the festival is the *kavadi*, or 'burden', which in its most extreme form consists of a large metal frame with several arcs and dozens of flexible metal wires piercing into the flesh of the penitent, acting as a bizarre parabola. Supported by four metal rods that hold the frame in place and attached to the body by a belt, the silver needles or spikes seem to criss-cross underneath the frame, finding one end in the flesh of the *kavadi* bearer.

Such a frame is also decorated according to the special preferences of the wearer, some with peacock feathers (in honour of the bird upon which Subramaniam rode), palm leaves, flowers, pictures of various deities, strings of wooden or plastic beads or bright plastic flowers, tassels, bells and anything else that devotees may see fit to carry as part of their offering. The frame is so heavy that thick, soft pads are placed on each shoulder to help bear its weight.

Silver needles or spikes, usually topped by a trident, may be used to pierce the tongue and cheeks; limes or small, round metal pots may be hooked into the flesh of the thighs, upper arms and other parts of the torso with fishhooks. Such an elaborate and penitential *kavadi* may weigh up to thirty kilos. Men, women and boys may carry a *kavadi* that is not as extreme as the above version, but it is mainly men who subject themselves to the physical rigours of flesh piercing (Hullet and Roces 1981:70).

Slightly less torturous forms of *kavadi* do not incorporate the large metal frame but are nevertheless strongly punitive. Devotees might have small silver containers of milk or have oranges or limes suspended from their chests and backs with fine silver hooks that resemble fishhooks, piercing the skin deep enough so that the hooks may hold the weight of the containers or

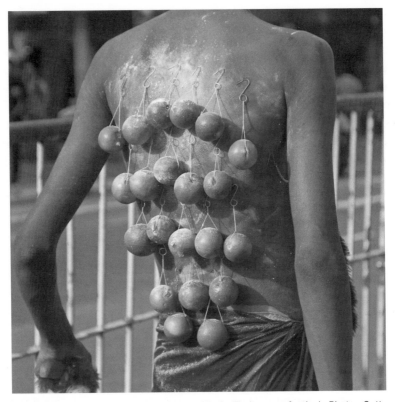

Figure 4.3   Limes hooked into skin at Hindu Thaipusam festival. Photo: Getty Images.

other objects. The *kavadi* vary in size from a brass jug of milk carried on the head and a light smattering of pins and needles inserted in the flesh to the extreme elaborate metal cage construction described above.

Different parts of the face might be inserted with hooks and spikes and decorated with delicate, linking chains. Like slim spears, the spikes are inserted horizontally through one cheek and out the other cheek and/or inserted vertically through the tongue. A silver trident, the symbol of Shiva, often forms one end of the spike that pierces through one cheek into the other. Once the needle is inserted, the trident is added for extra effect. Others might wear clusters of small needles over their whole body or walk the pilgrim trail wearing sandals with nails (Hullet and Roces 1981:71).

To endure these ordeals, the devotee maintains a complete fast twenty-four hours before donning the *kavadi*; then, dressed only in a yellow loin-cloth, he undergoes ceremonial purification and is smeared with sacred ashes to the accompaniment of prayers and clouds of incense. The combination of all these procedures induces a trance-like state intended to alleviate the pain. The *kavadi* is then attached to the penitent's body, the spikes, needles and fishhooks inserted, and he is ready for the pilgrim walk.

The atmosphere in the streets is charged with energy, colour, movement and the combined smell of rancid coconut oil, fragrant incense, sweating bodies and food. Crowds of supporters and onlookers chant, sway and shout their support; bright multicoloured Indian saris flutter about everywhere, and the streets are lined with festivalgoers and tourists.

Having walked the pilgrim route, the devotee prostrates himself before the statue of Murugan and then bathes in milk. He eats, and then the *kavadi*, the needles and the hooks, are carefully removed, and sacred ash is applied to the wounds. Although the bleeding is surprisingly negligible, there is still some blood flow. Once the Thaipusam is over, all who took part in the festival once again go about their normal lives until the next Thaipusam festival.

SADHUS

Sadhus[6] are India's itinerant holy men, thin ascetics, often with matted, dreadlocked hair and thick beards, who have surrendered family and social responsibilities as well as material possessions to pursue their spiritual search through meditation, devotion, the study of sacred texts and pilgrimage. Belonging to many different sects, their basic premise is devotion to a god, invariably Lord Shiva, and renunciation of physical pleasures which may lead to self-mortification.

Having renounced the world and its earthly pleasures and having turned their back on society and its rules in an effort to find *moksha* (salvation), they spend much of their time in meditation and prayer, moving from one place of pilgrimage to another or from one major festival to another. One thing they have in common is that they all long for union with the divine. Many sadhus are seen in the city of Benares (Varanasi), which has long been regarded as the city of Shiva Vishranath, the Lord of the Universe. Many engage in the constant repetition of the name of a god, or a powerful mantra can be internalized and synchronized with one's breathing so that the utterance of the prayer lasts until death.

Sadhus willingly endure great hardships and scorn clothing. Some appear red-eyed from the ritual smoking of hashish, and they may carry tridents in obeisance to Lord Shiva. It has been said that meditation hermits can be so lost in their meditations that birds sometimes build nests in their hair. Some have never cut their hair, and it reaches well beyond the length

Figure 4.4   Three Sadhu men, India. Photo: Lynne Hume.

of their bodies; others, however, shave or remove every particle of hair from their bodies or leave merely a tuft of hair at the back of the head. The way they wear their hair is as different as their apparel. Some wrap their heads with cloths or flowers, and some might wear turbans; some have beards and moustaches of different lengths and styles. Some wear marks on their foreheads that depict symbols of their beliefs; some practice harsh austerities such as standing on one leg for so long that the muscles in the other leg wither away.

Celibacy is the most important austerity practiced by sadhus. According to yoga metaphysics, sexual energy is the main potential source of spiritual energy. As an aid to mental control of sexuality, restraint and even physical punishment is sometimes employed. A *langoti*, a type of chastity belt made of wood or steel, is permanently worn by some sadhus. This austerity is usually undertaken for a minimum of twelve years. A *dhoti* sometimes covers the *langoti*. Displays of physical strength can be demonstrated in curious ways, such as lifting weights with the penis, sometimes weighing up to thirty kilos, also demonstrating the sadhu's transcendence of sexuality. The aim of this exercise is not to enlarge the penis but rather to desensitize the penis, to destroy its erectile capacity. Shiva is represented by the phallic linga (Shukla 2008).

A holy man might smear his body with vermilion powder, considered auspicious; others cover themselves from time to time in ash or ochre. Their feet might be barefoot or encased oddly in something very modern, such as a pair of canvas runners or old boots. Some carry a colourful cloth satchel that contains their very small possessions.

Many sadhus wear necklaces with beads that may be made of seeds called *rukaraksh* ('the tears of Shiva') and astrological rings. Through prolonged bodily contact, these ornaments are said to improve the physical and mental health of the wearer, including the relief of heart problems, high blood pressure and tuberculosis. Any *rukaraksh* necklace bought in Vishvanath Gali increases in power because of its association with the main temple, dedicated to Shiva in Shiva's own city.

Figure 4.5   Sadhu man, India. Photo: Dianne Osborne.

The Naga (naked) sadhus, or 'warrior-ascetics', belong to a large and prominent Shiva sect. The Nagas used to be extremely militant, fighting with rival sects, as well as Muslims and the British, and this warrior-like past is now visible in their display of weaponry: sticks, spears, swords and the trident, all of which nowadays have a symbolic function. Many Nagas still walk about India naked, even high up in the icy Himalayas. In their nakedness, they are said to control and inhibit sexual vibrations, retaining sexual energy to mystically transform its power into psychic and spiritual power.

Another type of sadhu comes from the small and obscure Aghoris sect.[7] Sometimes referred to as the 'crazy', god-possessed sadhus, they might emulate the most extreme characteristics of Lord Shiva as the conqueror of death, frequenting cremation grounds, smearing themselves with cremation ashes and sometimes wearing a garland of skulls and bones. The Aghoris willingly transgress all ascetic and Hindu taboos, believing that a reversal of values will enable them to gain enlightenment more quickly. While all sadhus are supposed to be vegetarian and teetotal, Aghoris eat meat and drink alcohol, often from a human skull, and eat the flesh of dead animals found in the street; they also might abuse people with foul obscenities. Stories abound of their eating excrement and the putrid flesh of corpses, drinking urine, engaging in ritual intercourse with menstruating prostitutes on cremation grounds and meditating while sitting on a corpse.

SIKHS

Sikhism[8] was founded in the fifteenth century in the Punjab, a part of northern India which is now in Pakistan and where the holiest Sikh shrine, the Golden Temple, is located. In the Punjabi language, 'sikh' means a pupil or follower, and 'guru' is a title for a respected religious teacher. Sikhism began with Guru Nanak (1469–1539), born of Hindu parents from the Kshatriyas caste (soldiers and rulers) in a village called Talwindi. From childhood, he was attracted to both Hindu and Muslim saints, and as an adult, he began to preach the message of unity of both religions. His teachings included the radical view that both the caste system and the ritual worship of gods in the form of *murtis* (icons or idols found in temples and Hindu home shrines) should be rejected. Sikhs use terms such as *accolade* or *service* to describe the respect that they pay to the gurus and other revered humans.

While Sikhism is monotheistic, it retains the Hindu idea of *karma*, that actions from one life affect the next life, and rebirth, with the soul moving through cycles of births and deaths. The goal of all Sikhs is to build a close and loving relationship with God through living a pure and honest life (*kirat karni*), meditating on the name of God (*nam japna*) and sharing through charitable work (*vand shakna*). They also believe that people of different races, religions or sex are all equal. The teachings of Guru Nanak were incorporated in the *Guru Granth Sahib*, the Holy Book of the Sikhs, comprising the teachings of the ten gurus from Guru Nanak to Guru Gobind. The fifth guru, Guru Arjun, built the Golden Temple at Amritsar which became the holiest of Sikh shrines.

The Five 'Ks'[9]

Their high moral character, courage and loyalty is symbolized by wearing the five 'Ks': *kesh*, *kangha*, *kirpan*, *kara* and *kachera*. *Kesh* means 'uncut hair'; Sikhs do not cut or trim their hair or shave and they wear turbans from about the age of eleven. The *kangha* is a small wooden or ivory comb, a symbol of cleanliness. The *kirpan* is a short sword or dagger reminding Sikhs of their duty to fight against evil and to defend righteousness. The *kara* is a plain steel bangle symbolizing one God and one truth, without beginning or end. *Kachera* are warrior shorts now worn as underwear; they symbolize leaving behind old ideas and following better ones.

The long hair is tied up in a *rishi* knot (*joora*) over the top front of the head, considered to be the solar centre for males (farther back on a woman's head), and covered with a turban, the *bana*, the primary identifying dress feature of the Sikhs, albeit not one of the five 'Ks'. The *rishi* knot stems from the idea that a *rishi* was someone who had the capacity to control the flow of energy and *prana* in the body. The *rishi* knot assists in the channelling of energy in meditation. If one cuts off the hair, there can be no *rishi* knot. A female Sikh may wear a *chuni* (chiffon scarf) across the head, under the chin and across the shoulder.

The 'k' item of clothing that is not publicly visible is the *kachera* (*kacha*, or 'breeches'), hidden as it is under the outward visible garments. Its functions have been variously described male protection, soldierly duties, control of the penis, and abandoning effeminate submissiveness or Hindu customs and superstitions (Singh 2004). The original form of the *kacha*, a thick, coarse cloth with many folds, especially in the front, provided a cushion that protected the most vulnerable part of the male body from any enemy blow in hand-to-hand combat. Sikh scholarship has focused on the *kacha* as a particularly male garment, but Nikky-Guninder Kaur Singh, taking a feminist approach to the *kacha*, argues that this undergarment is also important for women. Etymologically, *kacha* is related to *kacch*, which means 'underarm'. In Punjabi, the expression *kachh vicu varna* (literally 'stuck to an armpit') is used frequently

Figure 4.6   Sikh man holding child, India. Photo: Dianne Osborne.

to denote closeness between couples. Thus, the *kacha*, she argues, binds Sikhs in love and is in opposition to male dominance. By telling his Sikhs, both men and women, to wear the *kacha*, Guru Gobind Singh, in a very basic and innovative way, eliminated sexual difference (N.-G. K. Singh 2004).

Sikh Turbans[10]

During Guru Gobind Singh's time, Mughal aristocrats or Hindu Rajputs were the only ones allowed to wear ornate turbans, to carry weapons and to have a moustache and beard. The turban then was a sign of nobility and respectability.

It was in this context that Guru Gobind decided that all Sikhs should take up the name Singh ('lion') or Kaur ('princess'), boldly and fearlessly wear their turbans and carry a sword, which effectively made his followers see themselves on a par with the Mughal rulers.

The Sikh turban over uncut hair is a sign of a Sikh's complete commitment to live in complete accordance with the teachings. It is usually five metres of cotton cloth (coincidentally the same length of material as a woman's sari) and is considered to be much more than a mere covering of the head; the wearer gains a feeling of clarity and readiness for whatever the day may bring. The Sikh woman also wears a turban and may add a *chuni* (chiffon scarf) draped over her turban that extends across the shoulder and under the chin, which is said to protect the grace of the woman and to indicate that she is not sexually available.

Turbans come in every color and pattern, but there are three colours most commonly worn: white, deep blue and saffron orange. White turbans are said to be worn to extend the aura and the person's projection. Royal blue or navy blue are the colours of the warrior and are common among Sikh ministers, especially in India. Saffron orange represents wisdom and is commonly worn by Sikhs worldwide. Black turbans can represent surrender of the ego. Other colours of turbans do not have any specific significance associated with them (sometimes it is just a case of fashion, of matching a turban to a business suit, for example).

Some modern busy Sikhs, who do not want to take the time to wrap the turban around the head, resort to a 'Blue Peter' *Pag*, a prestarched turban which is tied round the head and left to dry. Once dry, the starched turban retains its shape and can be worn like a hat. Sikhs who reject the starched turban regard this practice as pure laziness and, more importantly, that the starched 'hat' detracts from the daily turban wrapping as a spiritual practice. One young man expressed it in this way: 'It feels fresher to tie it every day—it doesn't feel old, like three-day old boxer shorts' (J. Singh 2010:214).

Regardless of the circumstances or the type of employment or activity, a Sikh keeps his or her form and identity as a Sikh. Clothes are modest, immaculately clean and exemplary of the identity and character of a soldier-saint. Today, many Sikh practices are identifiable with Hindu practices, and intermarriages between the two communities are common. However, the Sikh community has its own unmistakable identity, and although Sikhs constitute less than 2 per cent of the Indian population, they are a visibly distinct element within the total Indian religious traditions and Indian society.

JAINS

Jainism[11] as a religious tradition was established in India about the same time as Buddhism, circa 500 BCE. Like Buddhism, Jainism rose against what some regarded as the corruption of the interpretation of Hinduism. The underlying philosophy of Jainism is the renunciation of worldly desires and the idea that self-conquest leads to perfect wisdom. Today, Jainism has more than three million adherents in India and finds wide acceptance because of its philosophy of sympathy for all living beings. Only a small minority of Jains renounce the world to pursue the ascetic path fully, but these are the most visible in appearance.

The focus of this religion is complete nonviolence, *ahimsa*, and the purification of the soul by means of right conduct, right faith, right knowledge and noninterference in other beings' spiritual paths. It is only through *ahimsa* that one can escape *samsar*, the cycle of rebirth. The cardinal doctrine of *ahimsa*, non-harm to any living creature, leads some Jains to wear thin muslin masks over their mouths to prevent them from accidentally breathing in small insects or to abstain from eating after dark in case insects should accidentally fall into their food and die. Some sweep the ground before them as they walk to avoid inadvertently treading on small creatures (Vallely 2009).

Silk, Silkworms and Natural Products

The notion of nonviolence extends to cloth or material made by harming or causing the death of any living creature: leather and skin for example which of necessity means the death of an animal and silk production which entails the killing of insects. Because of their strong commitment to not harming any living creature, many Jains do not wear anything made of silk, as it results from killing silkworms. In the caterpillar stage of the silk moth, the silk is secreted as a liquid from two glands in the caterpillar's head. For the production of silk, cocoons, still in their pupal stage, are placed in boiling water, which kills the silkworms and begins the process of unravelling the cocoons to produce silk thread. If allowed to develop and live, the silkworms would turn into moths and chew their way out of the cocoons to escape, resulting in much shorter and less valuable silk strands. Approximately fifteen silkworms are killed to make a gram of silk thread, and ten thousand are killed to make a silk sari.

However, there is a type of silk that does not involve such harm. It is called *ahimsa* silk, also known as peace silk, because it is produced without actually killing the silkworms.[12] *Ahimsa* silk production waits until *after* the moths chew their way out of their cocoons, thus allowing them to live. However, because of the chewed-through strands, less of the silk is useable for textile production.

Jainism's practice of nonviolence extends even to plants and the decoration of images of the *Jinas* (known as 'crossing-makers' because they made the 'crossing' from the material to the spiritual realm, from bondage to freedom). Any natural products such as flowers are only used if they have dropped from the plant naturally and not plucked; the buds of the flowers are not removed from their source. When making a garland of the flowers for the images, a needle is not used for stringing them together. The images themselves have to be cleaned with great care and handled with respect. While using a brush to clear the things stuck to the images of the *Jinas*, it should not make even the slightest noise. The flowers, the decorations, and the smearings which are used for various parts of the images should not be allowed to fall to the ground. In case they do fall down, they should not be used again, and they should be kept on a clean plate. If saffron is rubbed onto the idols, it must be done with a closed mouth, and when the saffron has been applied, the hands should be washed (Vallely 2009).

Jains who are neither monks nor nuns are referred to as 'householders', or lay Jains. They attempt to follow the doctrine of nonviolence in their lives but are not as strict in their adherence of this doctrine as are Jain monks and nuns, since complete *ahimsa* is not possible in everyday life. Some harm is inevitably done while preparing food, cleaning, walking, driving and other daily activities. While monks inculcate the virtue of total nonpossessiveness, householders merely minimize or limit possessions and are not attached to them. Some forms of employment are not possible for any Jain however, such as butchers, fishermen, arms dealers and even mill owners or wine merchants. They are also strict vegetarians.

Two Major Sects

Jains are divided into two major sects, the Svetambara (meaning white clad) and the Digambara (meaning sky clad, or nude), the division coming about mainly on the basis of dress and the interpretation of religious texts. Each of these sects is also divided into subgroups. Both groups accept the basic Jain philosophy and the precepts of nonviolence but disagree on details of the life of Mahavira, Jainism's spiritual founder, the spiritual status of women, whether monks should wear clothes, rituals, and which texts should be accepted as scripture. The philosophical differences between the groups mostly affect monks and nuns or the very pious.

Jain Holy Men and Women

Jain monks practice extreme asceticism and like other holy men take to the road completely nude or wearing a simple loincloth. Svetambara monks wear simple unstitched or minimally stitched white clothes and carry a begging bowl and a brush to remove insects from their path; they might also have books and writing materials. A loincloth which reaches up to the shins is called a *cholapattak*, and another cloth that covers the upper part of the body is called *pangarani* (*uttariya vastra*).

A woollen shawl that passes over the left shoulder and covers the body a little above the ankle is called a *kämli*. They also might carry a woollen bed sheet and a woollen mat to sit on. Those who wear clothes have a *muhapati*, a square or rectangular piece of cloth of a prescribed measurement, either in their hand or tied on their face to cover the mouth. They also have *ogho* or *rajoharan* (a broom of woollen threads) to clean insects around their sitting place or while they are walking. The use of wool is one of the areas of controversy within Jainism for, although taking the wool from a sheep does not incur violence *per se*, it may result in inadvertently harming the animal during the shearing process.

The Digambara sect is more austere and is said to be closer in its ways to the Jains at the time of Mahavira. Digambara monks believe that one can only lead the life of a true monk by having no worldly possessions and by demonstrating indifference to earthly emotions such as shame. They live completely naked, have no possessions, not even begging bowls, and so can only receive gifts in their cupped hands. This practice may vary among different sects of Jains, but the essential principle remains the same: to limit needs. They bestow their blessings on all, and some put *vakshep* (scented sandal dust) on the heads of people as they bless them. Digambaras believe that women cannot achieve liberation without first being reborn as a man, mainly on the premise that women cannot live a truly ascetic life because it is impractical for them to live naked. Digambara nuns are therefore clothed.

When a person renounces the worldly life and all the attachments and is initiated into monkhood or nunhood, the man is called Sadhu, Shraman or Muni, and the woman is called Sadhvi, Shramani or Aryä. Their renunciation is total, which means they are completely detached from social and worldly activities, instead spending their time engaged in activities for the purpose of spiritually uplifting their souls and guiding others.

Initiation

At their initiation, they take five major vows: absolute nonviolence, absolute truthfulness, absolute nonstealing, absolute celibacy, absolute nonattachment.

The *sadhus* or *sadhvis* should not even touch a member of the opposite sex regardless of their age; absolute nonattachment means they do not possess anything and do not have any attachment for things they keep for their daily needs. There are strict rules of behaviour about what food to eat, when to eat it and how it is prepared, as these can involve violence in some form; for example the cooking process involves violence in the form of fire and food preparation involves vegetable chopping, and *sadhus* or *sadhvis* do not want their own needs to be a part of the violence of another person.

They travel from place to place by walking, always with bare feet, no matter how uncomfortable this might be so that they can avoid crushing the bugs or insects on the ground. They do not stay more than a few days in any one place except during the rainy season, which lasts about four months, so as not to develop attachment for material things and the people around them. After receiving initiation, Jain *sadhus* and *sadhvis* do not cut their hair or shave their heads nor do they use a barber. Once or twice a year they pluck off their hairs or the hairs are plucked by others. This rather painful activity is called *keshlochan*, or *loch*, and is considered one kind of austerity because the pain associated with it is expected to be borne stoically and in a calm manner.

There are a variety of ways to be Jain, and while the ascetics form only a small portion of the large population of Jains, they highlight the focus of the Jain religion, which is nonviolence. Some contemporary young Jains might combine compassion with activism, protesting against the environmental crisis or world hunger (Vallely 2009:328). The focus still remains on nonviolence towards all beings, including oneself, and the eradication of suffering. Within the Jain population, like all other religions, there are degrees of adherence to strict principles, depending on the reality of engagement of individuals in a modern world and on the necessities of daily living in that world.

The religions covered here are but a small part of other religions, sects and numerous small groups focused around particular guru-style figures or holy people in India, as is the now worldwide religion of Buddhism, which is the focus of the next chapter.

–5–

The Buddha, the Dharma, the Sangha . . . and the Robe

The basic philosophy of Buddhism[1] is that one should lead a moral life, develop compassion, wisdom and understanding, and be mindful and aware of one's thoughts and actions. Buddhism is a religion of 'kindness and compassion', a sentiment that has been expressed many times by the fourteenth Dalai Lama of Tibetan Buddhism who refers to himself as a 'simple Buddhist monk' and his religion as a 'religion of compassion'. This sentiment is reflected in the Five Precepts of Harmlessness which are to refrain from intentionally killing any living being, stealing, sexual misconduct, lying, and indulging in alcohol and nonmedicinal drugs.

In practice, compassion leads to not harming any sentient being and striving to bring happiness to all beings. The 'triple refuge' of Buddhism is 'taking refuge' in the Buddha, the Dharma (Buddhist teachings) and the Sangha (Buddhist community of disciples). Wearing the robe not only communicates to the world that one is a Buddhist monastic but, above all, that the wearer is committed to high spiritual ideals, mastering the Dharma, liberating oneself and showing others the Way.

ORIGINS

Buddhism began about 2,500 years ago in India, with Siddhartha Gautama, a man from a wealthy family in an area that is now southern Nepal. On moving outside his protected environment for the first time, it is said that he saw 'four sights': a sick man, an old man, a dead man and a monk. The first three sights symbolize the human problems of sickness, senility and death, which all involve suffering (*dukkha*) and pain; the fourth sight—the monk—suggested a way of overcoming the problem of suffering. The Buddha's observations of the first three 'sights' made him question his privileged upbringing and assumptions about life, and he decided to renounce his home and family to look into the question of suffering. He took up the life of the mendicant, trading his fine clothing for the humble clothes of a mendicant seeker. Thus,

the basic monk's robe in Buddhist communities worldwide reflects the simplicity and humility of the mendicant seeker, and this basic robe underlies all
Buddhist attire in spite of regional variations. 'Taking the robe' became the
expression *par excellence* for entering the *sangha*, an outward and visible sign
of the monk's commitment.

EARLY ROBES

According to the Buddhist Scriptures and the Commentaries, in the early monastic days, the monks would go out on their alms-round dressed only in their
waistcloth which was neatly worn and carrying their upper robe and bowl in
their hands. When the monks were near houses, they would put on their upper
robe before going to collect alms.

Mendicant robes in the Buddha's time were made from discarded scraps of
cloth, or what is called in Sanskrit *pāmsūda* or *pāmsūla*. The wearing of 'cast-
off rags' was a display of ascetic humility which was a part of religious action,
along with living on alms, dwelling at the foot of a tree and using cow's urine
exclusively as medicine. There are various lists to identify what constitutes
pāmsūda, four of which are cloth that has been burned by fire, munched by
oxen, gnawed by mice or worn by the dead, highlighting the fact that such cloth
scraps came from the most impoverished and discarded of materials that
were scavenged from rubbish piles, found in the countryside, by roadsides, or
even from the cremation grounds, with the stench from garbage and the taint
and smell of death still on them. The Japanese equivalent of *pāmsūda* is a
term which can be translated politely as 'excrement sweeping cloth', indicating a potential source of the fabric (Karuna 2012).

The actual fabric was not as important as its humble origins, and it was of
no value to others; thus, a robe made of such material would not engender
covetousness or attachment. Any truly unsalvageable parts were trimmed off
and what was left was washed and dyed by being boiled with vegetable matter
such as tubers, barks, leaves, flowers and spices such as turmeric or saffron,
hence the origin of the term 'saffron robe'. It was then sewn into a rectangle large enough to wrap around and cover the mendicant. This most basic
bodily covering in those early times would have been a very simple rectangular
shape made of any kind of fabric in existence at the time.

The natural products available in India for dyeing fabrics resulted in a
variable and generic color of a reddish-yellow or brownish-yellow saffron or
ochre colour known in Sanskrit as *kāṣāya* (*kashaya*), denoting earth tones,

but which also means impurity or uncleanliness, referring to the source of the cloth used. Shades of this colour vary, and the use of an 'impure' or muddied colour was such an important feature that the word *kashaya* became the common name for the robes themselves. In Chinese, the term is *jiasha*, and in Japanese, the term is *kesa*.

The Sanskrit and Pali word for monastic robes is *civara* which generally has three parts (*tricivara*): an inner garment, which wraps around the waist to the knee like a sarong and ties at the waist with a flat cotton belt (*antaravasaka*); an upper robe, around the torso and shoulders (*uttarasanga*); and an extra outer robe that is used for warmth in colder climates (*sanghati*). With its double layer, the *sanghati* can also be spread out on the ground and used for sleeping, or it can be folded and worn over one shoulder. In addition to the three items worn by men, a Buddhist nun wears an additional vest or bodice (*samkacchika*).

The *uttarasanga* is a large rectangle, usually measuring about six feet by nine feet, worn wrapped around the body, covering one or both shoulders. While all three parts of the *tricivara* were made of *kashaya* fabrics, the *uttarasanga* came to be called the Kashaya Robe as it travelled to other countries. It has a fivefold or five-column rice-field pattern surrounded by a border. The rice-field pattern came about, it is recounted, because the living Buddha was asked to make a distinctive robe for his monks, and at the time, the Buddha was walking alongside a rice field in Magadha, so he chose the staggered pattern of rows in the rice paddy (*padi*) fields. Robes were then patched together in vertical columns, always odd in number, edged by a binding and to reinforce the material at the four outer corners, small square patches were used (Tanabe 2003:732). The paddy field patchwork notion has followed through in some branches of Buddhism but not all.

Traditionally, an ordained monk wore no shoes, but certain footwear was permitted for specific conditions, such as upper- and undersoles of wooden or leather sandals which protected the feet on rough ground. A thick wooden peg or leather thong, which can still be seen in India, holds the sandal in place between the first and second toes, said to press on certain nerves which control sexual desire. The traditional Indian sandals, with leather rings for the big toe and overstraps for the upper arch of the foot, are often seen in Tibetan *thangkas* (paintings or embroidered hangings) showing Indian Buddhist monks. Another type of footwear is a simple leather or cloth shoe, said to protect the wearer from snake and insect bites, leeches or again, when walking on rough surfaces. Another more effective style of footwear for protection in cold and in wet weather is calf-length boots (Beer 2004:227).

As well as demonstrating ascetic humility by wearing robes made of 'cast-off rags' another religious outcome associated with the robes is their effect on people in the laity. The Buddha permitted laypeople to give robes or the material for making robes to the monks. This gift of robes was thought to have the same beneficial karmic effects as did the giving of food to monks. In this way, the laity 'became joyful', because to give meant to receive merit (Mahāvagga VIII, 1, 36) and a better birth in a future incarnation. This practice led to robes being made of material other than rags; namely, cotton, linen, silk, hemp, wool and canvas.

Originally, Buddhist robes did not have any kind of fastening, but in order to maintain modesty on windy days, it is said that the Buddha permitted the use of cords and fasteners made of wood, bone or shell (Tanabe 2003:732). Buddhist robes can also function as devotional objects and amulets, becoming important as Buddhist relics if they were worn by great religious teachers, most especially if they purported to have been worn by the Buddha, about which there are many stories. Relics and other precious objects were sometimes sewn into the backs of the robes. Lay Buddhists sometimes made miniature *kashaya* to carry with them as amulets (Tanabe 2003:732).

The making of robes is prescribed in various texts and some strict lineages might insist on the specific manner of making, storing or donning a robe. For example, various texts recommend that each stitch be accompanied by a bow-ing gesture or an incantation, that robes be stored on high shelves among the perfume of flowers and incense, or that prostrations be made before putting on a robe. Before Japanese Sōtō Zen monks put on their robes, they 'make three prostrations, place the folded robe on top of their heads and chant a verse in praise of the robe as a garment of liberation' (Tanabe 2003:732).

Buddhist monastic robes of today are no longer made from discarded scraps, and the fabrics and colours differ from one culture to another and from one lin-eage, tradition or school of Buddhism to another, originally depending upon the local dye that was available in a particular region. Generally, the monks and nuns of the Theravada tradition in Sri Lanka, Cambodia and Thailand wear plain saf-fron or ochre robes. Theravada nuns in Thailand wear white robes; in Sri Lanka, they wear orange robes; in Nepal and Burma, they may wear a pink robe over an orange skirt, with a brown stole. In Korea, Vietnam and Japan, the robes might be black, grey or a pale blue; the ceremonial robes tend to remain as close to the brown-yellow or gold associated with the colour worn by the Buddha.

Nevertheless, in spite of differences in colour, donning the robe reminds all Buddhists of their commitment to the teachings of the Buddha. The robe is so versatile that in times of need, a part of it can serve as a blanket, a

Figure 5.1   Ritual shaving of a Buddhist monk, Bangkok, Thailand. Photo: Getty Images.

windbreaker or a head cover. As part of the Buddhist dress code for 2,500 years, it is perhaps the oldest style of dress still worn today. The robe is treated with great respect, and it is normal to undress by lifting it over the head, ensuring that it does not touch the ground. Similarly, sacred texts and teachings must be kept off the ground as a mark of respect.

Lay Buddhist clothing is indistinguishable from the dress of other people in any community; however, lay Buddhists are still expected to dress modestly and to behave according to Buddhist principles. Shoes are always removed at the entrance of any Buddhist temple or meditation area.

Figure 5.2 Chinese Buddhist monk in traditional dress. Photo: Getty Images.

BRANCHES OF BUDDHISM

Buddhism spread from India, where it originated, to China around the first century CE, and from there to Central Asia (Tibet and Mongolia), Southeast Asia (Burma, Cambodia, Laos and Thailand) and other parts of the world, most recently to the West. It is now a major religion in Japan, Korea, Mongolia, Taiwan, Bhutan, Sri Lanka and mainland Southeast Asia, as well as a minority religion in other Asian countries and is rapidly becoming the preferred religion of many Westerners. As Buddhism spread to different parts of the world, the form, colour and choice of fabric for the robe adapted according to region, culture, climate and the particular sect, tradition or school of Buddhism (principally Mahayana, Theravada and Vajrayana) and lineage of the wearer.

Buddhism in China

The cold climate in various regions of China necessitated additional layers, as the traditional triple robe did not provide enough warmth against bitter winds and freezing temperatures. As well, in Chinese culture, arms and shoulders were expected to be covered, not exposed. Chinese monks adapted the *kashaya* to suit both climate and culture by wearing robes with sleeves that fastened in the front, in the Taoist style, from close-fitting to 'dogleg' sleeves; colours of robes became muted in some areas and changed from one temple to another in different regions: yellow, light golden brown, brown, grey, blue, black and, in some epochs, purple.

Other Chinese cultural adaptations to the robe involved the functional and the political. Working in established gardens and fields was more to the liking of the Chinese than the practice of mendicant monks and alms-giving. This led to a more practical, labour-friendly type of dress and the adoption of wrapped leggings and split skirts in a culotte style to replace the lower robe or *antaravasaka*. The *kashaya* was only worn during ceremonial observances and meditation.

The political element accommodated the traditional hierarchical Chinese law and a system of rank developed in Buddhism in China. To indicate rank, the basic fivefold robe expanded to up to twenty-five strips of cloth, a larger number of folds and some very rich and expensive fabrics. Some ceremonial robes incorporated embroidered scenes in gold thread, a far cry from the original idea of a robe made from the scraps of material from dung heaps and cemeteries. Sleeved robes continue to be worn in China today, in a range of styles, with sashes and capes added.

Tibetan Buddhism

Elaborate and colourful Buddhist robes are found in Tibet and throughout the Himalayas, in the esoteric form of Buddhism known as Vajrayana. Vajrayana, writes Walt Anderson (1979:60), is Tantric Buddhism, which, at its essence, sees the fully enlightened human as a male and female being. A synthesis of the polarities of male and female is the highest goal of Tantric practice (Anderson 1979:62). The Sanskrit word 'tantra' is translated by Tibetans as a 'kind of thread'. The symbol of the weaving of threads is a metaphor for the interconnectedness of life and is a pervasive theme throughout Eastern spiritual disciplines. Although earlier forms of Buddhism probably arrived in Tibet as early as the fifth century, Vajrayana Buddhism was introduced into Tibet in the eighth century by a master monk commonly known as Guru Rinpoche.

Monks of the Gelukpa order, of which the Dalai Lama is the temporal head, wear yellow pointed hats, and in ceremonies such as exorcism rituals, lamas wear large helmet-like headdresses with crescent-shaped peaks. For initiation ceremonies, lamas wear crowns with five sections, each containing one of the five Dhyani Buddhas or the Sanskrit syllables that represent their essence. While wearing such a crown, the monk or priest summons up a particular deity, who may be depicted in a painting wearing a similar five-part crown. Within some Tibetan Buddhist schools, the most eminent monks, those considered

Figure 5.3   Tibetan Yellow Sect Buddhist monk. Photo: Getty Images.

to be living Buddhas, may wear their sleeveless tunic trimmed with a yellow brocade or wear yellow silk and satin as normal attire.

This clothing has a long history in Tibet, and in the early eighteenth century, an Italian Jesuit priest, Father Ippolito Desideri (1684–1733), who visited Tibet as a missionary, wrote meticulously detailed accounts of Tibetan apparel. As a dedicated Christian missionary, his writings indicate in no uncertain terms that he thought Buddhist beliefs and practices misguided at best, yet his detailed accounts of Buddhist clothing provide much information on the clothes Buddhists wore in the early eighteenth century (Sweet 2010).

Desideri noted that the 'special habit' for all religious devotees in Tibet was the same whether they were *lamas*, *rapjampas*, *gelongs*, or *drapas* or nuns (four ranks in Tibet). There was no difference, he said, between Tibetan monks' and nuns' habits and their ways of wearing them, and they were identical in colour and shape. Before donning the robes, a lama cuts and shaves the hair of the novices and gives them new names. His account of their 'habit' is as follows (note that the colour 'red' referred to is the same as 'maroon', and red and maroon are used interchangeably by monastics today):

> Their habit consists of a red cloth vest that comes down to the hips; it has no buttons down the center, but one part is laid over the other and secured at the hips with a sash of yellow wool loosely woven. The vest has no sleeves and leaves the arms entirely bare. It may be decorated with red, yellow or orange damask and with brocade for the lamas. When travelling they are allowed to wear another kind of vest of the same colour with sleeves, to protect against the cold.
>
> From the hips to the heels, the form of the habit resembles a very wide woman's skirt, sewn along its length so that it has no side opening, hemmed at the bottom, and with the upper part not sewn, so that it must be gathered together at the hips. The skirt is brought over the hips and folded over itself a number of times both front and back and then secured over the hips by another sash, like the one used for the vest.
>
> The soutane or skirt described above is not made of thick material like the vest but of a quite fine red-coloured cloth resembling the finest, most beautiful and most delicate European carded wool; it must be doubled for greater modesty. (Sweet 2010:327)

He noted that neither the monks nor the nuns were permitted to wear trousers. When travelling they were sometimes allowed to wear 'a long padded garment tied at the hips and lined with leather on the lower part', and could also wear

> a large yellow woolen cap shaped like the crown of our hats, with long lappets of the same wool extending behind and over the ears to the nape of the neck that

are generally worn folded up to where they hang from the cap. They do not wear this hat when reciting prayers or when they visit their lama when they wear a different cap, also of yellow wool, but worked in such a way as to resemble yellow velvet. From the forehead upward is triangular in shape, and in the back and sides from the forehead down to the shoulders it is square-ish with wide fringes of yellow wool. This type of large cap is worn on the head or over the left shoulder, with half of it hanging down in front and half in back. (Sweet 2010:328)

Both inside and outside the home in place of a cloak, they wore over their shoulders 'a sen [*zen*] of red cloth that resembles a long blanket, neither too wide nor too narrow, the middle part which is worn over the head like a veil, with two ends hanging down on both sides in such a way that one end is thrown over the left shoulder, the other end crosses under the neck and down the chest, from the right shoulder to over the left' (Sweet 2010:327). With regard to their footwear: 'Both indoors and outdoors they wear boots that reach to the knees. The part that covers the foot is made of well-tanned white leather, and from the foot to the knees it is made of red cloth ornamented with beautiful silk and embroidery work, especially around the top of the boot' (Sweet 2010:328).

Robes in Tibet Today

Robes worn in Tibet today, as will be seen in the following paragraphs, seem not to have changed at all from the accounts given by Father Ippolito Desideri, and range from very simple to highly elaborate and colourful, from a bright yellow to maroon, to a vibrant purplish red. The large, distinctive head coverings worn on special occasions continue to be worn, and there is no distinction between the robes of monks and nuns, apart from the extra clothing worn by women for modesty.

The hat and special cloak worn at monastic assemblies are also described by Venerable Geshe Rabten in his autobiography (2000): 'the cloak must be made of two parts sewn together' and a 'band of lotus markings is sewn beneath the collar; below this many folds run down the length of the cape.' The upper part of the cape symbolizes Buddha Shakyamuni's teaching, and the lower part represents the teachings of Buddha Maitreya. The two parts are sewn together to symbolize that there is no gap in time between the 'destruction of the first and the rising of the second' for those who continue their practice from one era to the next. The intention is to bring 'all sentient beings to the bliss of enlightenment', symbolized by all the folds leading to the lotus petals on top. It is only essential for a monk to wear this cloak and hat at monastic assemblies (Rabten 2000:45).

Rabten also comments on the significance of the boots referred to by Father Ippolito above. The shape of the monk's boots, he writes, is a reminder to the wearer of the three 'mental poisons': attachment, hatred and confusion, represented by the rooster (attachment), the snake (hatred) and the pig (confusion). All the suffering in the world arises from these mental distortions, and it is imperative that they are eradicated. The 'curved-up tip' of the boots resembles a pig's snout, and on both sides of each boot are two 'bumps', resembling the upper part of a rooster's wing. The curve from the top of the boot to its tip is said to resemble the curve of a snake (Rabten 2000:42).

The skirt-like lower garment, continues Rabten, is to remind the monk of his vows and the duties resulting from his ordination. The borders at the top and bottom of the garment symbolize that a monk should live within the bounded community of a monastery and engage in study and meditation, helping to cast off the suffering of the round of existence and gain the joy of liberation. The folds of this garment are highly significant, symbolizing the four truths of superior beings: on the right side are two folds facing backwards, symbolizing the two truths to be abandoned (suffering and the cause of suffering) and on the left side two folds face frontwards, representing the two truths to be attained (the truth of cessation and the truth of the path which leads to that cessation). The harmonious practice and unification of method and wisdom is needed in order to abandon the first two truths and to attain the latter two; this is symbolized by the two folds facing each other in front (Rabten 2000:43). These instructions are also given to nuns at their ordination. Thus, the robe reminds the monk (or nun) not only of his or her ordination but also of the necessity to practice method and wisdom together as aspects of the Buddhist teachings.

The understanding of impermanence is a very important Buddhist concept, and in order to remind the monastic of impermanence and the inevitably of death, on each side of one of the upper garments (the vest) are two pointed main streaks crossing each other by the armpit and meeting at a point. These represent the jaws of the Lord of Death, and the middle of the vest is his mouth symbolizing that the wearer lives between Death's jaws, liable to die at any moment.

Thus, the monastic robes are highly symbolic garments and when worn with the proper motivation and understanding of their significance act as constant reminders of the path chosen by the wearer. What is most important is that the wearer's attitude, mindfulness and way of life be in accordance with the meaning of the symbols. If monastics put on their robes each day with full awareness the symbolic meaning of their clothes will remain with them for the entire day.

Figure 5.4   Buddhist monks, Cambodia. Photo: Dianne Osborne.

Buddhist Nuns in Australia

The following comments of some Australian Buddhist nuns[2] highlight not only their feelings about donning the robe for the first time at ordination, but also how the symbolism of each part of the robe is highly significant to their way of life. Note that Tibetan terms are used for each of the parts of the robe: the maroon lower robe/skirt is *shemdap*; the shirt with elephant-ear-shaped sleeves and lapels is the *dhonka*; the shawl worn on the upper half of the body is the *zen*; the underskirt is *meyo*; the undershirt without sleeves, which is usually yellow, is *ngülin*; the yellow robe with large tiles worn for teachings and other formal situations is *chögu*.

Venerable Lhundub Tendron, who was ordained in 2002, said that the robe is always treated with respect as a sign of the vows made at ordination. 'As your feet are regarded as a dirty part of the body, you put the robe on over your head; you do not step into it and you don't put your robe on the ground; this would be disrespectful.' This was reiterated by Venerable Lhagsam, who was ordained in 1977, and Venerable Lozang Drolkar, who was ordained in 2011.

All three women viewed the robe as a form of 'protection' and a 'reminder of what they want out of life': to follow the Buddhist monastic path and to be 'mindful'. Tendron said it made her 'very happy to wear her robes'; Lhagsam said she 'would not want to *not* wear her robes' as 'our robes remind us of our vows'. Drolkar, the most recently ordained nun, commented that on the first time she went out in public after her ordination she 'felt nervous':

> People stared. I kept looking forward, happy they could get the imprint of the robes—the imprint of an ordained person, the imprint of something virtuous. But that was about my 'self-cherishing'. Robes are liberating—you don't have to think about what to wear. You don't spend time and effort on unimportant things. It keeps you respectful, mindful.

The notion of 'imprint' appears in the discussion of Lama Zopa Rinpoche, after a waiter in a restaurant where he was having lunch commented on how he liked the robes and wondered where he could get one. Rinpoche commented that it was due to 'Dharma imprints' that the waiter was drawn to the robes. Someone so drawn to the robe might possibly have been a Tibetan monk in a past life (Rinpoche 2005:20–22).

At ordination, a nun is dressed by other nuns, and this is the first time that she puts on her robe. On this occasion, Drolkar said she was too preoccupied with her thoughts and the ordination itself to think about the robe, but after the ordination, she said it 'felt unusual, but an honour' to be dressed in her robe. 'But in the end', she added, 'they're "just clothes". It is not the clothes themselves but what they represent that is important'.

Colours that are specifically not worn by Tibetan Buddhists are black, white and green. Nuns at the Chenrezig[3] Buddhist community in Australia wear maroon and saffron-coloured robes, following Tibetan tradition. They also have a thin blue piping around the edge of the *dhonka*, which has a specific story associated with it. It is said that in the ninth century, King Langdarma assassinated his younger brother, Ralpachen, the king who had helped to develop Buddhism in Tibet. Langdarma ruled for many years after the death of Ralpachen, and during Langdarma's reign, he tried to eradicate Buddhism. Interestingly, it was the Chinese who came to Buddhism's assistance this time. When the Buddha's rules of discipline were almost wiped out, three monks escaped to Amdo, near the Chinese border, wanting to revive the practice of ordination there. However, to be fully ordained, there have to be five monks present, so they invited two Chinese monks to join them. At that time, Chinese monks wore blue in their garments. The additional piping that is seen today on the Tibetan Buddhist robes is added to the robes in order to remind Tibetan Buddhists of the help given to them by the Chinese monks.

Footwear among Buddhists in the West varies according to climate, availability, and, to some extent, comfort. Some of the Chenrezig nuns wear sandals, shoes or even sneakers, as long as the colours are as close to maroon or brown as possible so that they do not detract from the overall appearance. The right arm is usually bare to symbolize 'non-grasping' after material things and is a sign that the person is always ready to give a helping hand to anyone who needs it. (While showing a bare arm is acceptable in some countries, in others it is culturally inappropriate.)

All dress has to be neat and 'presentable' in appearance to convey the impression of an ordered mind and a happy and ordered life. New robes are generally purchased from a Buddhist country overseas or made by a local dressmaker in a store-bought fabric. At Chenrezig, they have a box of old secondhand robes which are given out to any nun in need of extra or replacement robes. The old robes might have a tiny tear in them, but this can be mended or hidden in the folds of the robe. One of the nuns in the community acts as a robes manager. Lhagsam said that the first time she put the robes on by herself she found them 'a bit complicated', especially 'the skirt part as it is a big piece of material like a tube, which you put on over your head'. There are, she explained, 'two folds in the skirt going backwards, representing two truths to be discarded: suffering and causes of suffering, and there are two folds that are folded forward, representing the true cessation of suffering and the true path and practice of dharma'. Over the tube skirt, you can use a cord or a strip of cloth for holding it all in place. The 'skirt has a border at the bottom and a border at the top, symbolic of not going beyond the vows and of maintaining the moral conduct expected of a Buddhist monastic'. Under one's robes, she added, one is not to wear 'trousers' or tights, even if it is cold. However, socks are permissible. They wear no jewellery, though watches might be worn sometimes for practical purposes. 'The Chinese,' she said, 'use a clasp to hold their robe in place but we don't.' She said that the day after her ordination when she had to remember instructions about putting on the robe she didn't do it very well, and a monk said to her, 'Ani-la, that's no good' and told her how to adjust the robe to make it 'sit right'. 'Robes', she said, make you 'act differently, you are mindful of proper behaviour'.

If the weather is really cold and necessitates additional warm clothes, such as a pullover, they must be worn inside the *dhonka* as wearing them outside 'looks messy'. It is not acceptable to wear the *zen* wrapped around the head or thrown carelessly over the shoulder or around the neck. This is perceived as very disrespectful. To show respect to a teacher, one must always lift and hold the long end of the *zen* respectfully. When the Dalai Lama visited Chenrezig in 2011, monks and nuns assisting him would always cover the hand that was to touch the Dalai Lama, with their hand covered by their *zen*.

Specific instructions given by Lama Zopa Rinpoche (2005:20–22) with regard to how this should be done are as follows:

> As you enter the room you lift the end of the *zen*, from on top of the right arm and draw it back across the shoulders respectfully. [. . .] As you sit in the teaching you can spread the long part across your lap and hold your hands respectfully in your lap, the right hand loosely held by the left.

He added:

> Although the *zen* wrapped around the right arm is considered disrespectful in the Tibetan tradition, it is the style of the Theravadins, so it's OK for them, you shouldn't get upset with them.

Also, if a hat is worn, it must be taken off in front of a guru or senior monk. One must sit respectfully, no leaning on walls, no stretching the legs toward the guru or altar; hugging the knees is disrespectful. Such actions can create negative karma.

Wearing the robe is for life. The vow to not separate from the robes is the 'morality of intermediate ordination of renunciation'. The robe communicates to everyone that

> Buddhism is something that doesn't harm others, that benefits and brings peace to others; something that offers wisdom and compassion, not demanding blind faith; something very profound, deep. (Rinpoche 2005:21)

OTHER ITEMS OF DRESS

As well as the robes, hat and boots mentioned above, there are other items of dress that pertain to monastic attire. For example there is a small bag which monks take to a monastic assembly at which tea is to be served. The bag has a leather drawstring, the touching of which is a reminder that it was once the skin of a living animal, again the notion of impermanence. (Not all Buddhists are vegetarian, and when begging one accepts all that is offered. If someone is sick, meat might be required in their diet. They may also use leather in dress.) This small drawstring bag has the four colours of the elements: blue, red, yellow and white that represent air, fire, earth and water. Buddhists believe that consciousness depends on these four elements that make up the body, and if the connection between these elements and consciousness is broken, death results. From the bottom of the drawstring bag to the top, the colours are blue, red, yellow and white (Rabten 2000:47). By seeing these colours, one is reminded of the dependent relationship between these physical elements and life.

Mala

A ubiquitous item of dress that accompanies Buddhist activities is the *mala* (Sanskrit for 'garland' or 'rosary'), and the Buddhist equivalent of the Roman Catholic rosary beads. The *mala* enables the monastic to count mantric recitations, prostrations and other devotional practices; so in essence it is a counter. The *mala* is a string of 108 even-sized beads and can be made from many different materials: seeds, sandalwood, bone and crystal are the most popular (Thurman 1995). As a multiple of 12 and 9, the number 108 represents the 9 planets in the 12 zodiac houses. Although a *mala* might be made of other numbers of beads, 108 is used by most practicing Buddhists.

There are, however, specific types of beads recommended for specific rites. For example in the 'peaceful rites of appeasing', while the beads should still number 108, they should be either clear or white in colour and made of crystal, pearl, mother-of-pearl, white lotus seed, moonstone, conch shell or ivory. In the 'enriching rites of increase', the beads also number 108 but should be made of bodhi seed, lotus seed, gold, silver, bronze or copper. In the 'magnetizing rites of attracting or drawing power into one's sphere of personal influence', the beads should number twenty-five and be made of red coral, carnelian, red sandalwood or saffron-scented redwood. In the 'wrathful rites of destructive or forceful activity', the beads should number sixty and are made from *rudraksha* seeds, human or animal bone, iron or lead. While other types of beads are now used, the traditional bodhi seed and red sandalwood are thought to be universally auspicious for all practices. A cautionary note about the use of human and animal-bone *malas* is proffered: these should only be used by accomplished yogins, as karmic influences are believed to be inherent in ritual objects made of bone (Beer 2004:215).

The string used to make the beads into a *mala* is traditionally wound from three to nine individual strands; three representing the Three Jewels of Buddha, dharma, and sangha, and nine symbolizing Vajradhara and the eight bodhisattvas. A single strand is not used, as it might suddenly break. Traditionally, the thread should be spun by a young virgin girl belonging to the tantric lineage of the specific Buddha family (Beer 2004:215).

The *Kata*

The *kata* is a greeting scarf that is offered to the lama at the beginning or end of most Tibetan rituals. Usually white and made of cotton or silk, it derives from one of the most ancient customs of Indian culture, wherein a guest was offered clothing or 'precious raiment' (Thurman 1995:104). It is often seen being given out, or being received, by the Dalai Lama.

RANK AND HIERARCHY

In spite of the simplicity, humility and, one assumes, equality advocated by the Buddha with regard to Buddhists, rank and status crept in as Buddhism spread far and wide over time. In East Asia, additions in dress designed principally for warmth began to reflect status differences between both individuals and different monasteries, indicated principally by the use of colour. Within medieval Japanese Zen monasteries, for example, ordinary monks wore black under-robes and *kashaya*, while abbots wore robes of colour, and deep-purple robes were only the prerogative of abbots of a senior monastery of the highest status. Colder climates in East Asia and different customs resulted in tailored garments worn beneath the *kashaya*.

In the twentieth century, some Japanese under-robes have crests that symbolize particular sects or scenes from the life of the sect's founder. Also in Japan, the folded *kashaya* vary in style according to sect. They are worn across the chest in the Nichiren school, or sect, and as circlets around the neck in the New Pure Land sect. In 1561, the New Pure Land sect decreed that their monks would wear white under-robes for happy events such as weddings, black under-robes for solemn occasions such as funerals and coloured under-robes for other ceremonial functions. Laypeople also wear the abbreviated *kashaya* around their necks as badges of affiliation and piety (Tanabe 2003:734).

By the sixth century in China, under-robes consisted of an upper garment that had neckband sleeves falling to the wrist and a piece of pleated cloth used for a skirt. In East Asia these two pieces eventually were sewn into a single kimono-like garment. In Japan, a culotte-type skirt was also worn. *Kashaya* were no longer needed just for warmth and modesty but were used to convey rank, status, occasion and sectarian affiliation. Ecclesiastical ranks were assigned certain colours and mirrored those used at the imperial court (Tanabe 2003:732).

Many high-ranking monks in East Asia wore *kashaya* made of exquisite brocades decorated with gold leaf, gold threads and embroidery, justifying such rich choices of fabric as being marks of respect for the garment itself. During the seventeenth to the nineteenth centuries in Japan, laypeople donated fragments of bright and richly decorated theatrical garments for monks to patch together for robes, thus still maintaining the original notion of patchwork from scraps of fabric (Tanabe 2003:734).

Cultural differences will no doubt continue to change as Buddhism wends its way across the world. Large numbers of people in Western countries have wholeheartedly embraced Buddhism. Buddhism in the United States is becoming more Americanized, with monks and nuns tending to follow the colour code associated with their teacher's tradition, often wearing their robes over the top of ordinary clothes. One person suggested that American Buddhist robes might even be made in blue denim in the future. As fabric changes have been modified throughout the world, this might not be as surprising as it sounds. As long as the blue denim takes into account the patchwork motif, perhaps this could happen.

THE ROBE AS DEVOTIONAL OBJECT

After the Buddha's enlightenment under the bodhi tree, he taught for forty-five years, and undoubtedly, in this span of time, he would have worn a number of different robes, some of which were handed down to others, and over time even disintegrating pieces of cloth from these robes became relics, about which there are many stories. Robes of other great religious teachers might be passed to their disciples as 'evidence of transmission of the teachings', and function as proof of spiritual lineage. Occasionally, robes and other valuable objects will be deposited within *stupas* (reliquaries). Sometimes relics and other precious objects were sewn into the backs of robes, and pieces of a robe might be carried around as amulets (Tanabe 2003:734).

As can be seen, the Buddhist robe, with its swathes and folds, can symbolize simplicity or splendour, equality or rank. No matter how it is worn, the robe is full of symbolic meaning, mirroring the ideals of Buddhism. In spite of the variations in colour and nuances of style according to cultural differences and climate in the various regions of the world, throughout Buddhism the most basic emphasis with regard to all dress and accoutrements is simplicity and the avoidance of any hint of ostentation.

In the end, to wear a Buddhist robe with true Buddhist intent, the colour, style or number of layers is not important. Buddhism is a religion of compassion, a way of life whose quintessence is nonattachment, even to the robe. To 'put on the Buddha's Robe' is to make a statement about belief. This is summed up by Master Lin-chi I-hsuan, the founder of Rinzai Zen, who lived in the ninth century CE and who is said to have made the following statement:

I put on various different robes . . . The student concentrates on the robe I'm wearing, noting whether it is blue, yellow, red, or white. Don't get so taken up with the robe! The robe can't move of itself; the person is the one who can put on the robe. There is a clean pure robe, there is a no birth robe, a *bodhi* robe, a *nirvana* robe, a patriarch robe, a Buddha robe. Fellow believers, these sounds, names, words, phrases are all nothing but changes of robe . . . Because of mental processes thoughts are formed, but all of these are just robes. If you take the robe that a person is wearing to be the person's true identity, then though endless *kalpas* may pass, you will become proficient in robes only and will remain forever circling round in the three-fold world, transmigrating in the realm of birth and death. (quoted in Karuna 2012:3)

BUDDHISM AND DEATH

Buddhism does not prescribe any particular preparation of the corpse or type of funeral so this will vary depending on cultural traditions. Cremation is common, though Chinese Buddhists prefer burial.

Dying Buddhists may request that all pain-killing or other drugs, which impair clarity of mind, be withdrawn shortly before death. Buddhists would usually have no objection to an autopsy, though most Buddhists would prefer that the body be left in an undisturbed state for as long as possible. Mahayana Buddhists prefer the body to be left untouched for up to eight hours, while Tibetan Buddhists usually wish it to be undisturbed for three days. After a Buddhist has died, his or her relatives will often perform acts of generosity or religious observance in the person's name and dedicate the power of that goodness to the well-being of the deceased.

Tibetan Buddhists have very explicit and detailed practices surrounding dying, death and caring for the body and soul of the dead person. It is not important how the body is disposed of, because in effect it has just become an empty shell once the consciousness leaves the body. However, this might take up to three days while it is going through the final stages of psychological dissolution; if the body is disposed of before consciousness has left it is considered to be very disturbing for the person. During the process of dying, there are certain procedures for caring for the dying person, and once deceased, for guiding the dead person through the intermediate state and into a good rebirth.

As recounted in *The Tibetan Book of the Dead*, when a person dies a white cloth is thrown over the face of the corpse, and from then until it is deemed that there has been a complete separation of the *Bardo* (the after-death state) body from the physical body, the corpse remains untouched, which may take three to four days; doors and windows are closed and a mystic chant is performed (Evans-Wentz 1973:18–28). An astrologer-lama is consulted to cast a death horoscope based on the moment of death and to determine the proper method of disposing of the corpse.

After the corpse has been removed from the house for final disposal, in some cases a tradition is to make an effigy of the deceased from a stool or block of wood and dressed in the clothes of the deceased; over the effigy's 'face' is placed paper upon which certain symbols have been drawn: a central figure representing the deceased, a mirror to symbolize the body, a conch shell and a lyre to symbolize sound, a vase of flowers to symbolize smell, holy cakes to symbolize essence or nutriment and taste, and silk clothes to symbolize dress and the sense of touch. The effigy is offered food until forty-nine days after death, the time when the principle of consciousness is said to re-enter a body or some other world according to its karmic consequences.

These Tibetan rites are believed to predate Buddhism and to pertain to the ancient, pre-Buddhist Tibetan religion of Bön, thought by some to resemble in many ways the religious rites of the ancient Egyptians. At the termination of the funeral rites, the face-paper containing the aforementioned symbols is burned in the flame of a butter-lamp and the spirit bade farewell, at which time the clothes of the deceased are given to the lamas to dispose of as they think fit. The ashes of the face-paper are mixed with clay and made into tiny *stupas*, one of which is kept for the family altar and the rest placed in some protected location, such as a cave or a hilltop.

When the corpse is ready to be removed from its house, the officiating lama presents a 'scarf of honour' to the corpse, advising it that it is dead and that its ghost must not haunt or trouble living relatives. As the lama begins to lead the funeral procession, he takes hold of one end of the long scarf, the other end having been tied to the corpse, and begins to chant a liturgy to the accompaniment of a miniature hand-drum and a trumpet made of a human thighbone. Other sounds come from a handbell, a conch shell, brass cymbals and the chanting of the lama.

The human body is said to consist of four elements: earth, air, fire and water, and the corpse needs to be returned to these elements. Final disposal of a corpse is varied; it may be buried in the earth, given air burial, cremated or cast into large bodies of water such as a river. The most common type of disposal appears to be cremation or air burial. When birds have stripped the bones of the flesh, the remaining bone pieces are pulverized and mixed with a powder to allow birds to complete the air burial.

On rare occasions, a corpse may be embalmed. When a body is cremated, the ashes, hair and nails are placed in either Buddha images or *stupas* (reliquary monuments). However, as *The Tibetan Book of the Dead* was translated from the Tibetan into English in 1927, the traditional practices do not necessarily apply today, given the spread of Tibetan Buddhism elsewhere in the world since then, and with the Chinese occupation of Tibet.

Within the practices of Burmese Buddhist villages, the male members of the family take the dead body to be washed and wrapped in burial clothes. The thumbs and big toes are tied together with hair from a deceased member of the family. A coin is placed inside the mouth and at the head; a vase is placed holding a flower so that the dead may still worship Buddha. The body is never left alone from the time of death until cremation. The conscious soul is believed to remain in or around the body for up to three days. The body can be cremated only after this time. On the seventh day after a person has died, monks are invited to the deceased's house to chant from the sacred texts in order to confer merit upon the soul of the dead person and to encourage the ghost to leave (Kramer 1988:54).

In the next chapters, we take a leap in another direction. While still focusing on the religious body, Part III considers dress that has distinct associations with the mystical and the magical. Beginning with Chapter 6, three quite different groups, which are not ordinarily considered together, are discussed because of their commonalities with regard to the more esoteric aspects of religion and their differences from mainstream religious practices.

PART III

THE MYSTICAL AND THE MAGICAL

–6–

Sufis, Indigenous Shamans and Modern Pagans

Each of the groups discussed in this chapter are uniquely different to one another, yet they all call on, and incorporate, both internal spiritual practices and external methods of achieving an altered state of consciousness that leads to a metaphysical outcome. Sufis open a metaphysical 'doorway' into a spiritual world in order to merge with the Beloved, shamans move into trance in order to access spiritual realms so that they may heal or gain knowledge, and modern pagans use both individual and group magical practices and ritual to 'work magic'. All three groups dress and use tools and/or actions that accord with their specific set of beliefs. 'Dress' becomes an intrinsic magical/mystical part of their practices.

SUFIS

A mystical offshoot of Islam, Sufism focuses on the qualities of tolerance, forgiveness and enlightenment, and the attainment of a deep love of God. The name Sufi comes from *suf* (wool) and refers to the woollen garments worn by the earliest Sufis who proclaimed that, by purification of consciousness, the self and God could merge. Sufism is probably best known through one particular group, the Mevlevi Order of Sufis, named after its founder, Turkish mystic poet Jelaluddin Mevlevi Rumi (1207–1273). They are also known as the Whirling Dervishes, the term 'dervish' meaning 'doorway'; the whirling movement in their dance ceremonies assists the Sufi to pass through a metaphysical doorway into a spiritual world to merge with the Beloved.

The symbolism of the robes is central to the mysteries of the order. The black robe (*kirqah*) symbolizes the grave, and the tall camel's hair hat (*sikke*) represents the headstone. Underneath are the white dancing robes consisting of a very wide, pleated frock (*tannūr*), over which fits a short jacket (*destegül*). On arising to participate in the ritual dance, the dervish casts off

Figure 6.1 Whirling Dervish, Turkey. Photo: Getty Images.

the blackness of the grave and appears radiant in the white shroud of resurrection. The head of the order wears a green scarf of office wound around the base of his *sikke*.

The *Sema* Ritual

The elegant and mystical whirling dance that is contained in the Sufi *Sema* ritual is part of a person's spiritual journey to perfection through intelligence, love and the abandonment of the ego. Every nuanced movement and article of clothing reflects the spiritual focus of a dance that is imbued with sacredness and accompanied by mesmerizing, evocative music.

The *Sema* ritual consists of a *shaikh* or dance master (*semazenbashi*) and dance participants (*semazens*) and is held in a ceremonial hall. Whirling, or turning, symbolizes the cosmological concept that everything in the universe revolves and that no matter in which direction the dancer faces, he is always in the presence of God.

At the commencement of the *Sema*, the dance master, who is understood to be a channel for the divine grace, stands in the centre, the place of Mevlana Rumi, awaiting the arrival of the dancers. He is dressed in all white, with a white felt hat (*sikke*) and white shoes. The dancers (*semazens*) wear traditional dress: a *tennure*, a sleeveless white frock, a *destegul* (literally a bouquet of roses), and a long-sleeved white jacket, with the right side tied down and the left side hanging open. Around the waist is fastened the *alif-lam-and*, a girdle of cloth that is similar to a cummerbund, and a black overcoat or *khirqa* to be removed before the whirling begins. The voluminous white skirts symbolize the ego's shroud. On their heads is a *sikke*, a tall, tan-coloured camel felt hat, representing the tombstone of the ego. In addition, a turban is sometimes worn, which is wrapped around the head. On their feet they wear black shoes (Ernst and Lawrence 2002). The black cloak worn at the beginning of the dance represents the restrictions of the material world, and when it is dropped to the floor, the dancer symbolically leaves his tomb of worldly attachments to reveal wide bell-like skirts, which begin to billow as the dancer turns, enabling him to focus his attention and to prepare himself for his blissful merging with God.

The dance begins with the Sultan Veled Walk, a circular procession three times around the ceremonial space to the accompaniment of hauntingly beautiful *peshrev* music. The dancers bow to each other during the procession, recognizing that they are 'face to face', 'essence to essence', 'soul to soul', honouring the spirit within each of them. As their arms unfold, the right hand opens to the skies in prayer, ready to receive God's grace, and the left hand is turned towards the earth in a gesture of bestowal of that grace to earth.

Whirling is punctiliously executed by the feet. The physical axis is the left leg and foot, revolving 360 degrees with each step; the right foot crosses it to propel the dancer around and around, just as the universe turns around and around. While continuing to maintain awareness of their movements, the dancers twirl on their own physical axis, counterclockwise, twenty to thirty times a minute, making small, controlled movements of head, hands and arms, while silently repeating, 'Allah, Allah'. Their bodies are straight, their heads inclined slightly and their flowing white skirts make a triangular pattern that is meant to be maintained throughout the ceremony (Ernst and Lawrence 2002).

Emptied of all distracting thoughts and thinking only of God they lose themselves in total surrender in one-pointed concentration on the one Reality, whirling in timelessness and spacelessness. The entire sacred performance is a graceful display of precision movement carried out to the sounds of mystical Turkish classical music. If a dervish should become too enraptured, another Sufi, who is in charge of the orderly performance, will gently touch his frock in order to curb his movement.

Four musical movements (*selams*) are involved in the dance, each with a distinct rhythm, beginning and close. In the first *selam*, the human being's birth to truth through feeling and mind is represented; in the second *selam*, the rapture of the human in front of God's greatness and omnipotence is expressed; in the third *selam*, the rapture of self dissolves into love; the dancer experiences the intensity of the annihilation of self by way of elimination of ego, to merge with the Beloved, expressed poetically as, 'Together we fly through the heavens of Being to merge with our Creator' (Helminski 2006). In the fourth *selam*, the descent back to the physical world, the dancer returns from the spiritual journey. The journey completed, the individual is able to love and serve the whole of creation more easily, having experienced the bliss of divine love.

The *Sema* is both a form of worship and a meditation in movement, in which the dancer is the axis, integrating all levels of being within himself. When the ceremony is over, the dancers once again don their black cloaks to represent their return to the material world. The ceremony then ends with a prayer for the peace of the souls of all prophets and believers.

INDIGENOUS SHAMANS

Shamanism[2] might be said to be the earliest form of religion. Certainly, there is evidence that a form of shamanism was practiced in the 'deep past' when humans lived in caves and painted or incised cave rock faces, and in various forms, shamanism continues to be practiced in many different areas throughout the world. Shamans are mediators, communicators and messengers between the world of humans and the world of spirits, and provide important spiritual and holistic healing services to their people, assisting in the return of lost souls to their physical bodies, providing advice on medicine and restoring balance to the individual and the community.

In many places, dress is an important part of the outward sign of the shaman's ecstatic journey, with parts of the dress displaying the helping spirits that are called upon to assist the shaman on trance journeys. In this way, the dress becomes an agent of transformation (Maginnis 2004:57). In many parts of Siberia, apprentice shamans must learn how to make their own shamanic outfits, with the guidance of both human and spirit teachers.

The model of a multilevel cosmos, reported in a simplistic manner as consisting of three major realms or worlds (Upper, Middle and Lower) is represented symbolically and pictorially as a tree, the *axis mundus*, with its roots in the Lower World, its trunk in the human everyday world and its branches reaching up high into the Upper World. A journey to one realm might start with a soul ascent from a high place, such as a tree, a mountain and so on; a journey to another may begin with the soul descending into a cave, a body of water, the roots of a tree or other natural passage that can take one downward into the earth.

The tree, or a pole, may be used to ascend via its branches to the Upper World, or descend, via the roots, to the Lower World (Townsend 2004).

The shaman's dress reflects his or her otherworldliness and connection with the natural world and the spirit worlds in a variety of ways, depending upon the culture and the geographic region in which he or she lives. In one Siberian tribe, the Goldi, when there is talk that a new shaman has appeared on the scene, the question asked is: 'Yes, but has he got the costume?' making explicit the importance of the shaman's dress to his authenticity and suitability for the role of shaman. In this part of the world, the shaman may inherit the costume or he may have it made for him, but it is a necessary part of becoming and being a shaman (Vitebsky 2001:83).

Dress, including tools and other paraphernalia, vary from one region to another; some are highly elaborate, others extremely simple. An Amazonian shaman who closely identifies with the jaguar as his helping spirit might wear jaguar skin along with necklaces of jaguar claws and a hollowed jaguar bone that contains his hallucinogenic snuff (Vitebsky 2001:46). A North American shaman might wear a necklace made of grizzly bear claws symbolizing the power and fierceness of this animal, while a Siberian shaman might wear an antler hat to imitate the powers of the deer and to assist him to move swiftly or to ride it into the Otherworld. He might embellish his garment with soft attachments and dangling pieces such as fur fringes, soft leather, beads and reflective surfaces such as pieces of mirror and cover his face to protect himself from malevolent spirits.

Elsewhere, the shaman might wear a macaw hat, a boa-skin jacket, rayfish trousers and armadillo feet to move about in the realms of air, earth and water (Vitebsky 2001:91). Feathers can be employed for similar purposes, that is, to have the characteristics and facilities of whichever bird they represent. Masks are worn in some places and even cloths to cover the shamans' eyes to activate their inner sight.

The Other Realms can be dangerous places, fraught with monsters of various kinds, and the wearing apparel of the shaman helps to protect him, imbued as it is with the magical and physical qualities of his nonhuman helpers. The bones, skins and sinews of dead animals might be procured so that the shaman can breathe life into them in order to send them on missions of accomplishment to bring about a result, and these items may appear on or be incorporated into his dress or paraphernalia.

Although power objects are not actually a part of the shaman's dress, objects such as a medicine bundle of dried herbs, a dried bear's paw, a bunch of feathers tied to a drum or an animal effigy can form part of the shaman's overall dress. Alaskan Inuit shamans called such an effigy a *kikituk*. Secreted somewhere on his body, it was said to enter and leave his body through his mouth or armpit carrying out tasks such as biting a patient's harmful spirits and sending them on their way or killing an enemy by burrowing into his heart. A small and lithe animal, it was said to 'peep out through the corpse's mouth, under the arms and through the ribs' (Vitebsky 2001:84).

Universally, shamans are regarded as having special powers not possessed by ordinary folk and are usually viewed and treated in a different manner to other members of the community. There is invariably something about his (or her) persona that sets him apart, and he is often reported as having a special light shining from his eyes (Berndt and Berndt 1977) or a gaze that can pierce into a person's thoughts.

As in life, so in death which might mean that the corpse of a shaman is given special treatment and extra care as his power possibly continues into the afterlife. He (or she) might be buried cross-legged and with his hands in a position of prayer, facing in a particular direction (north, in the Himalayas), and the tools he has used in his shamanic activities are buried with him. In Nepal, a shaman's corpse might be buried beneath a cairn of rocks, and his tools and other paraphernalia, including his outfits, are hung on a nearby tree. His most important item, his drum, would be slashed and silenced (Vitebsky 2001:95).

Drums and Sounds

Although drums are not used in every shamanic community, they are the most universal sound-making tool of the shaman, enabling him to call on the spirits and to enter the trance state (Czaplicka 1914; Potapov 1999; Vitebsky 2001). The shaman's drum is most often round, with stretched animal skin covered with esoteric symbols and animal figures and decorated with fur, feathers, fringes or beads, but this varies from one culture to another. In some places, the fabrication of the drum is a meticulous operation and can be a magical act. The drum is important not only because it helps the shaman to enter a trance state, but also because it may be used as a mount, a boat or a container to scoop up spirits. All the time he is performing his magic, he is in constant movement, sometimes standing, sometimes crouching, or twirling, dancing, or hopping from one leg to the other.

The sounds accompanying the shaman's dress and tools are as important as the shaman's visual appearance and dress might incorporate bells and metal ornaments about his body or sewn onto his dress, so that he is impressive not only to look at but also to hear. Metals such as iron, brass and copper may take abstract shapes that represent nonhuman beings as well as abstract items.

The sounds of such embellishments, such as the tinkling of bells, the clinking of beads and buttons, or a rattling sound from other items, add to the strangeness of his dress and his overall magical appearance. In Siberia and Mongolia, metal ornaments, made by the local blacksmith, were essential attachments to the shaman's regalia, and their sounds were heard at his slightest movements. The Samoyed shaman (*tadibey*) tied a handkerchief over his eyes to penetrate the spirit world by his inner sight (Czaplicka 1914; Maginnis 2004).

Symbols on the shaman's garb are implicit with symbolic meaning. Contemporary Siberian shamans might wear a coat, a mask, a cap and a copper or iron plate over the chest; his coat may have fringes around the sleeves or the neck below the collar and slits ornamented with cured leather. Both the slits and the fringes have been reported as representing the 'curves and zigzags of the Milky Way' (Czaplicka 1914). Various amulets, serving both a magical and a decorative purpose, might be made of skin and beads and fastened to parts of the dress by the shaman himself.

Chants, spells, invocations or prayers form part of the sound repertoire, creating a mystical or magical effect. The shaman cuts an impressive and terrifying spectacle of sight, sound and movement; always the audience has the expectation that something awe-inspiring is about to happen.

The Nepalese shaman summons spirits by beating his round drum and calling to them, slowly at first, and then more forcefully, until there is a crescendo of thunderous intensity with loud drumming, singing and calling to the spirits, their arrival announced to the audience through the drum being hit hard and purposefully, at which time the shaman adds a breastplate to his costume while

> with the most diverse sounds, from thunderous beats with the sharp clang of iron to the most delicate rustling, a continuous soft hum, accompanied by a light jingling . . . in the darkness it seems as if his voice moves from one corner to another and from below to above and back again. (Vitebsky 2001:54)

The audience is captured and enchanted through sight, sound and the smell of smoke, animal skins, food being prepared, and the sweat from bodies. The shaman himself must be a frightening sight to behold as his actions are sometimes accompanied by physical manifestations such as convulsions, foaming at the mouth, eyes that might be glazed or turned upwards, and loud breathing as he moves into a trance state. The whole dramatic shamanic rite is an intensely sensual experience, but it is also a performance with a purpose: to contact the spirits and to bring about an outcome.

Korean Shamans

In most places, the shaman is a male, but in Korea, the shaman is invariably a woman and is known as a *mansin* or *mudang* (Kendall 1985; Kister 2004;

Figure 6.2   Korean shaman dressed for ritual. Photo: Getty Images.

Maginnnis 2004). At the start of a ceremony called *kut*, performed outside and in public, which calls on the spirits of the ancestors to possess her body, she arrives on the scene with a repertoire of bright clothing pieces, robes, tall head-dresses over a firm headband, and other paraphernalia, producing an extraor-dinary splash of colour, deep blues and reds predominating but also electric pinks and purples. An altar displays rows of neatly stacked colourful fruit, such as oranges, and throughout the entire performance, she is accompanied by a supporting troupe of singers/musicians producing a cacophony of sound from their voices, metal drums and gongs.

At times, she swirls, twirls and jumps, perhaps flashing metal knives or picking up flags made of several metres of colourful fabric, or she may hold a fan, representing dignity, in one hand, and in the other a cluster of jingling bells. Once she has entered a trance state, the spirits enter her body. During a trance, she might dance with long pieces of material which she deftly incorporates into her movements.

She wears layers of dress and is ready to change her clothing during the course of the ceremony, depending on which spirits appear. All the extra clothes are worn over her main basic clothing, and as each spirit speaks, dances or acts out through the *mansin*, she switches garments, since the spirits are thought to inhabit the robes. Certain outfits are associated with particular types of ancestor spirits, and the *mansin*'s voice, demeanour and attitude change to reflect their characters (Kister 2004). They may be spirits of great kings, mountain gods or other regal personages whose dress is wide-sleeved red robes and tall hats or a greedy government official whose garment is a blue vest and broad-brimmed black hat. When the *mansin* puts on a yellow robe, the culturally attuned audience knows that she is possessed by a demanding spirit grandmother, while a yellow blouse and red skirt pertain to a princess or maiden who is angry because she died before marriage or before having a child (Kendall 1985; Maginnis 2004).

There are an endless array of spirits and accompanying outfits. As the spirit who comes through to temporarily inhabit the *mansin*'s body may be either male or female, the *mansin* has to adapt her body mannerisms, dress and voice to match. During a typical *kut* ceremony, she becomes a sexually liminal being, at times male, at times female, and sometimes a child. Children who died before they became adults may cry and demand sweets and are indicated by tying a child's robes to the belt of the *mansin*. During the performance, she may engage in amazing feats of endurance such as balancing barefoot on razor-sharp knives (Kister 2004).

There is also an element of farce and comedy in the Korean *mansin*'s performance, and in her role of male spirit, she may tell rude jokes and argue with the audience in a way that would be unthinkable for a woman in the normal public domain (Kister 2004). Her changed personality and dress allow this to happen in a ceremonial context. The spirit robes and headdresses of a Korean shaman are usually stored in the *mansin*'s shrine when not in use (Maginnis 2004:60).

MODERN PAGANS

Alternative systems of belief have existed alongside mainstream religions for millennia and are sometimes forced underground by more dominant religious beliefs, resurfacing more publicly again during liberal political regimes. Because of the permission of freedom of thought in Western countries, there has been a resurgence of alternative beliefs throughout the Western world since the latter part of the nineteenth century. Religions of re-enchantment have surfaced in response to the emphasis on science, materialism and pragmatics. The number of contemporary pagans, consisting of magicians, Druids, pagans and Wiccans, has burgeoned since the 1950s, when there was a resurgence or more public revival of witchcraft and occultism in England. In their modern form, they are now scattered throughout North America, Europe and Australia.

Modern pagans[3] have a rich repertoire of mystical-magical dress that symbolizes both the natural world and the spirit world. The body is generally viewed as something to be honoured and celebrated rather than hidden and regarded as a source of shame. In one pagan subgroup, Wicca, a poetic address to the Goddess appears in the Charge of the Goddess, written by Doreen Valiente: 'Let my worship be within the heart that rejoiceth; for behold, all acts of love and pleasure are my rituals' (Valiente 1978; Hume 1997). The human body in all its forms, shapes and sizes is honoured and celebrated.

Pagans display their 'magical selves' through clothing, cords, jewellery, talismans and magic bundles, highlighting their fascination with the fantasy worlds of myth and magic. Body adornment ranges from painting the naked body to covering it with animal skins and fur, adorning it with flowers and leaves, or helping it to disappear under a hooded robe.

Modern Paganism, sometimes referred to as Neo-Paganism, is polytheistic and animistic. On the basis of putative ancient pagan beliefs and rituals which have been adapted or created, Paganism reflects influences from a variety of sources: Neoplatonism, alchemy, Freemasonry, Rosicrucianism, spiritualism, theosophy and, more currently, ecological concerns and enchantment.

Rather than being structurally organized from a central place, or governed by any unique person of authority, Paganism can be described as a segmented, polycentric integrated network system because of the nature of its structure. Its followers meet in small groups, some of which gather together during the year for major festivals or conferences such as the Wiccan Conference. There is no building or fixed sacred structure such as a church, synagogue or temple; rather, sacred space is created anywhere, either outside in nature or in private homes.

Paganism is a religion of enchantment and magic, and dress includes an amazing array of fantastic clothing, ranging from the flimsiest transparent outfits to full-length, heavy velvet-hooded capes, medieval garb, face paint, headdresses, jewellery, curved pointed boots, other fancy footwear and anything else that captures people's imagination. To attend a major festival with pagans from all the various subgroups (for example Druids, Wiccans, heathens) is like stepping back into the Middle Ages or into the pages of a fairy story, with elves, fairies, dragons, wizards and witches all there, along with other

fantastic characters. The type of dress is only limited by the individual's imagination. Women are often seen at a pagan gathering wearing corseted, floor-
length medieval-style dresses of any colour, often in velvet with lace trims,
which are invariably worn under heavy medieval-style velvet-hooded robes
during a ritual. Men's clothes often consist of trousers with drawstrings, a
T-shaped tunic that falls to mid-thigh, in linen or cotton, over which is the
hooded robe, but again, men's dress can be as wide in scope as their ability
to employ their imagination.

A subgroup called the Fairy Tradition attempts to achieve altered states of
consciousness by putting people off balance, twirling and spinning until dis-
oriented. Their clothing can range from wearing fairy wings to dress that reflects their own version of creatures that might appear in fairy stories. Some
groups create a synthesis of history and Hollywood, from Goths that dress entirely in black, wearing heavy white make-up, black lipstick and nail varnish, to
vampires who look as if they have just stepped out of a Dracula novel (Hume
1997:55). Rituals are replete with astounding visuals, sound and dancing and
always the air is thick with the smoke of incense and melting candle wax as
participants fully engage in ritual activities.

Clothing, or lack of it, is closely linked to pagan cosmology. Ritual nudity,
'going skyclad', is regarded as a natural state of being which allows freedom
from inhibitions. The skyclad body also indicates the casting aside of social masks and roles, honouring the sacredness of each and every body and
placing all on an equal footing regardless of the size, shape and flaws of the
individual body. Although the majority of people remain 'robed' at pagan festivals, some dance skyclad around the sacred circle during a ritual. The body
is viewed as a divine gift, to be celebrated rather than subjected to self-denial
and punishment as it is in some religions. It is believed that the divine is im-
manent as well as transcendent, and all acts of love and pleasure are simply
one way of celebrating the divine gift of the body. Hence, there is no notion of
a sinful body that must pay penance to become worthy.

As well, some believe that the naked body imparts some sort of odic force
or animal magnetism which may assist in the raising of power within the
magic circle. More commonly however, casting off everyday clothes is akin to
casting off the mundane and doing away with social roles and expectations.
Nudity also asserts that the body is sacred and needs no adornment; whatever the size and shape of the body, within the sacred circle, all bodies are
considered beautiful and are honoured as sacred to the goddess and god.

The most basic item of dress which cuts across most of the various subgroups of Paganism is the black hooded cotton robe. In its most simple form, the
shape of the robe resembles an *ankh*, the ancient symbol of life, with the flared

sleeves forming the horizontal bar of a T-shape and the hood the rounded loop of the cross. The traditional black robe enables the wearer to 'disappear' into the night if disturbed by nonpagan voyeurs, which can sometimes occur, as many rituals are performed outside in forests, woods or other natural surroundings.

As well as basic black, the robe can be any colour, selected according to individual preference and the particular ritual to be performed. Many robes are made of cotton, hemp, velvet or satin, and some have highly elaborate symbols incorporated on to the fabric, the five-pointed star, or pentagram, is particularly relevant to Wiccans. Silvery-grey satin robes might represent the moon, the goddess and feminine energy; gold represents the sun and the god and masculine energy; colours and designs might reflect the four elements of earth, air, fire and water: earth is associated with greens and browns, red with fire, blue with water and yellow with air, but this may vary, and personal taste decides from among a vast array of combination, colours and designs. Various shades of purple are associated with the mystical and the magical; purple is a popular colour among both males and females, and purple velvet is ubiquitous at pagan gatherings and festivals. Pagans in general display their 'magical selves' in a diverse number of ceremonial garments that reflect myths and fairy stories.

Worn over the robe is a floor-length cape, frequently made of velvet, crushed velvet or cotton, with long sleeves flared towards the wrists or no sleeves but with two slits so that the arms may go through to enable movement. The cape's hood is usually large, so that it drapes slightly onto the neck, giving it a medieval appearance. Pagan ritual places importance on connecting with the energy of the earth, so the feet are usually bare during a ritual to more easily make that connection.

Depending upon the climate, clothing fabric may vary from heavy wool, velvet, and fur-trimmed capes to summer-weight cotton, silk or hemp, if one favours natural fibres, especially groups or individuals who focus principally on nature, to synthetic materials, shimmering, diaphanous and bejewelled clothing for those leaning to a more magical look of enchantment. Amulets and talismans make up part of the ritual adornment; amber, crystals, amethyst and black jet are often worn in necklaces and other forms of jewellery.

The pentagram, the five-pointed star, is *de rigueur* for Wiccans, especially in the form of a silver pentacle worn around the neck or as a ring; sometimes it is tattooed on the body or embroidered onto a cape or robe. Runes, gems and goddess images are common, and many rings are worn on the index finger of the dominant hand, regarded as the 'power finger' for working magic. Headbands and armbands are sometimes worn; for women, headbands in silver and set with a crescent moon with upturned horns (a symbol of fertility), and for men gold headbands set with a sun may be seen. But again, there are many other symbols used in jewellery, on clothes, and as decorations in the hair, and in the preferred footwear. The latter shows a love of fantasy and enchantment: from leather thigh-high boots to ankle boots, shoes and slippers in felt, satin or cloth, some with upturned pointed toes, others made specifically to accompany whichever fantasy mode articulates their magical persona.

Cords and garters may serve different purposes. Garters might be made of velvet, snakeskin, leather or lace; cords are knotted to accord with the initiations the person has undergone and are a specific length. The *cingulum* (a long cord or cords), generally linked with esoteric initiations, is worn around the waist over the robe. Dress depends upon several factors: individual preference, the pagan subgroup to which they belong, the seasonable celebrations and particular rituals.

Hair is associated with strength, vitality and psychic protection, and in folklore, a witch's magical powers were thought to be bound up in her hair; some think that letting the hair flow loosely at a certain point in a ritual can aid in the power of a spell. In telling contrast to many of the religions already discussed, where hair is the part of the body that is the focus of a woman's 'looseness' and therefore needs to be controlled, long, flowing hair is preferred by women and men, and women often dye their hair red with henna, indicating freedom from restraint and too many rules.

Masks may be used in certain rituals in order to assume a different persona, according to the particular focus of the rite. For example, Samhain, 31 October in the northern hemisphere, is the Festival of the Dead, known by other religions as All Saints' Eve. It is a time of winter darkness, for sadness, for remembering ancestors, but it is also part of the cycle of birth, death and rebirth. It is said to be the 'time when the veil between the worlds is at its thinnest'. Clothing for Samhain is usually dark or black, reflecting the sombre darkness of winter, and the ritual often incorporates a death figure, dressed in whichever way the group feels represents the anthropomorphic notion of Death, to remind each person of the inevitability of his or her own demise.

The whole gamut of what it is to be human—birth, growth, sexuality, life, joy, disappointment, sadness, death, decay and vitality—is incorporated into pagan celebrations and discussions. Other cyclic rituals, *esbats* and *sabbats*, similarly enact seasonal ceremonies, some reflecting the colours of the natural environment, plants, flowers, greenery and sentiments of the particular passage of the seasons. Dress for a spring rite incorporates spring colours to reflect the lightness and promise of spring after the long darkness of winter. Garlands of flowers often encircle the heads of women, and men might appear as 'green men' or other characters from myths and folktales.

Pagan dress might also be further embellished by items from the natural environment. As well as flowers, dress might include leaves, bird feathers, animal skins, bones, teeth, fur and even large antler horns for specific rites. A special ritual might completely obscure the human body, so covered is it with masks, headgear and bodily paraphernalia, giving it the appearance of an other-than-human being and totally transforming the wearer. Ritual dress can appear spectacularly impressive at night in a natural environment under a full moon, or at the dark moon, with the only light coming from the fire in the centre of a circle and a multitude of candles.

Rituals based on specific myths call for different dress, as in the enactment of the Greek myth of Demeter and Persephone, described by Ezzy (2011). The story of Persephone's descent into the underworld was vividly brought to life in this ritual enactment, allowing participants to experience their own metaphorical death through the mythic tale. Images, clothing, face-masks, body painting, the smells of the earth and smoke, of burning incense, the sounds of drumming, the emotional anticipation of not knowing what was to happen created an air of excitement in a highly charged atmosphere. Black, loose clothing under capes and robes were worn by most, while role-players of the deities Hecate, Hades, Persephone and Demeter wore lavish outfits and heavy make-up that contorted faces and transformed them into surreal personages. The awesome spectacle of tall, dancing black-robed figures swinging as they whirled to the accompaniment of loud drumming contributed to an overloading of the senses and trance states for many participants. Dress contributed to the overall effectiveness of the experience, allowing participants to address the reality of their own mortality.

Sara Pike (2001:189) describes another pagan festival, this one held in the United States, which captures the sense of group ritual participation:

> As they walk differently and dance differently, festival goers claim that the body is transformed, and so they also say, is the self . . . Costumed, tattooed, jewel-covered, and glistening nude dancers, chanting, drummers and other musicians, smoke, and flame, make festival fires a feast for the senses.

Clothing becomes imbued with ritual smells from incense such as frankincense, smoke and charcoal smells from the centre circle fire, and oils ritually placed on people as they enter a sacred circle. Rituals performed at night, sometimes at full moon, sometimes at dark moon, become a truly magical event for participants, invoking all the senses. Creating an aura of mystery and magic is important to pagans as it aids in changing one's consciousness, and they dress in a way that will promote this change.

Apparel, in general, indicates to all present that for a short space of time, they move out of the mundane world. Rituals are designed to enable practitioners to enter a magical world via the imagination, trance and ceremonial acts. The sacred circle, within which rites are generally performed, is a space set apart for the sacred, and before one enters such a space, one establishes the appropriate mind-set, does the necessary preparations and dons special dress so that the person's ordinary life is left far behind.

Clothes worn only during rites are said to build up their own special energies and contain their own magical substances. A robe worn to many rites over several years contains an accumulation of energy and becomes very special to the wearer. Just to pick up a robe that has absorbed the smells and 'energy' of various rituals is enough to put a pagan practitioner into a special frame of mind that engenders a sense of anticipation or memory of a past magical ritual.

The smells of incense such as frankincense, the waxy smell of candles, oils that are ritually dabbed on participants as they enter the sacred circle, and smoke from the central fire are all absorbed into the clothes of the ceremonial participants and remain there long after the ritual is over. The word 'perfume' comes from the French term *per fumar* which literally means 'from the smoke'; smells from smoke were once considered to be the souls of objects and thus spiritual and sacred in themselves (Johansen 2010:47). If left unwashed, the smells absorbed by ritual clothing can last for many months, sometimes even years. When rituals are performed outside in nature, there is invariably the smell of the earth, perhaps wet and rotten leaves, wet ground, seasonal natural smells, animal smells, flowers, and so on. The clothes and their smells become themselves magical and can induce a trance state, or a preparatory setting that can take pagans into the appropriate mind-set for trance to occur, the smell evoking memories of past rituals.

Ritual dress includes necklaces, earrings, rings, bracelets, toe-rings, headbands, amulets (protective charms) or magical tools and accoutrement such as wands, staffs, *besoms* (brooms) and *athames* (symbolic sword or knife). The pentagram (five-pointed star) or pentacle (five-pointed star within a circle), which is highly symbolic and imbued with meaning, is the symbol that expresses pagan cosmology at a glance. Four of the points of the pentagram represent the elements of earth, air, fire and water, with the fifth representing spirit. The pentagram is employed ritually, within the sacred circle, and is the typical sign to denote Wiccans.

Celtic knots and other designs on dress and jewellery are also highly favoured among certain groups. Meaningful symbols, such as the crescent moon, the pentagram, and Celtic symbols, may also be tattooed on the body. Tattooing, body paint and make-up serve to reinforce significant symbols and to create a special readiness to transform oneself within a sacred space from the mundane to the magical. Some have tribal designs or depictions of their 'familiars' tattooed on their bodies. Face make-up serves to extend dress on to the face and to create an immediate impression of 'other'; magical eyes can be created through cat's-eyes contact lenses, heavy black kohl liner and glitter, endowing the wearer with an alien or otherworldly appearance.

Depending upon any particular ritual, whether one of the seasonal cycles, a 'handfasting' (pagan wedding) or a ritual to perform a specific magical 'working', participants' dress and accoutrements incorporate all the senses: the feel of the sacred space, the touch of the robes on the skin, the smell of lit candles, smoke, fragrant incenses and oils, the sounds of different creatures in the environment (if held outside), ritual music, whether that be drums, flutes, songs, or recorded music, and the emotional intensity of the ritual itself. As with the seasons, birth, marriage and death are viewed as transitions, a necessary cycle, with each one being celebrated and connected with the otherworld. Pagans are annually reminded of death at Samhain, where they dress according to how each individual person feels is appropriate. Reminders, such as photos and mementos, of friends and relatives who have died before them are often placed on the altar and/or set up on a special table which has been set aside for that purpose. In some subgroups of Paganism such as Wicca, someone dressed in black and wearing a death mask might move around the sacred circle facing each person present, silently confronting them with the reality of their own demise. Once death occurs, each pagan has his or her own ideas about what is done with the corpse and how it should be dressed, constrained only by the legal requirements of their country or ethnic background.

In all metaphysical matters and practices, dress is a reflection of belief, an essential item whether it is dress or undress, and an aid in the practices themselves. However, quintessential to the magical and the mystical is the *inner* experience, the *inner* journey. That is the heart and spirit of the pursuit.

The next chapter takes us further into the metaphysical, with the experience of possession, where the 'spirit' moves into the body of the practitioner, with dress being an expression of that embodiment.

Possession: Vodou, Santería and Candomblé

Vodou in Haiti, Candomblé in Brazil and Santería in Cuba are all African-derived religions, their roots traceable to West and Central Africa (see Bodin 1990). Oppressed by a system of slavery intent on effacing their humanity, black people uprooted from Africa slowly evolved their own religion, based on their African heritage, which created a communal bond that served as the secret foundation for their various struggles for freedom.

In spite of regional variations since the displacement of millions of black slaves to the New World, these religions share commonalities in belief and practices: human–spirit interaction and interdependence, relationships based on the reciprocal exchange of services, possession and blood sacrifice.[1] The latter might seem abhorrent to Westerners, but to these practitioners, blood is an essential element as the living energy that is released is believed to feed and form the spiritual world. Ancestor worship, active participation in ceremonies and the employment of highly charged drumming and dancing create an exciting atmosphere for these vivid and vibrant religious ceremonies where people and spirits are bound together spiritually, personally and communally.

The practitioners of Vodou, Candomblé and Santería venerate a number of distinct spirits, invisible forces of life generically referred to by each of these religions as *lwa/loa*, *orixá* and *orisha*, respectively. In the Fon language spoken in Benin, one of the tribal groups living in that area of Africa that is home to the Hausa and the Yoruba, *vodun* means an invisible force, terrible and mysterious, which can meddle in human affairs at any time. They therefore need to be propitiated in the correct manner (Bodin 1990; Hurbon 1995).

VODOU

In Vodou[2] ceremonies, participants worship a pantheon of ancestral spirits who are intermediaries between the living and the *Gran Met* (God). Such ceremonies consist of a riot of dazzling whites and bright colours, high-energy drumming that reaches a furious pace at the height of the ceremony and exuberant movement and trance dance, all conducted within a spiritually charged space for the express intent of spirit possession of a human body. Sweat-drenched bodies, food smells, perfumes and the odour of animals to be sacrificed all pervade the ceremonial area, and the sounds from chanting, songs, drums, rattles and colourful swaying clothes and petticoats all add to the sensuality of the Vodou ceremony (Deren 1970 [1953]; Tselos 2000).

A Vodou service might be held for a number of reasons, such as the celebration of a seasonal festival, for an initiation or a funeral, to honour a spirit or to address the life problems of a congregant. If a *lwa* is satisfied with the way it has been honoured, it will confer power and advice; if dissatisfied, it can enact punishment. During such a ceremony, the *lwa* is said to 'ride' or 'mount' its human recipient, who is referred to as a 'horse'. As the *lwa* enters the body of the 'horse' the individual invariably reacts with a shudder or convulses for a short time until the divine possession takes place, when the 'self' of the person moves aside for the duration of the possession. Everyone present recognizes which particular *lwa* is present through its mannerisms, personality, likes and dislikes, and speech (Deren 1970 [1953]; Hurbon 1995; Tselos 2000).

Once the transference has taken place, several high-ranking initiates assist the possessed 'horse' to dress in sacred garments that have been consecrated for the express purpose of their use by that particular *lwa*. Dressed in these garments the enculturated audience recognizes the dramatic change that has taken place, the change of garments visibly signifying the *lwa*'s presence (Tselos 2010). After being dressed, the *lwa* proceeds with counsel, admonishments and words of wisdom for those present. The garments are worn for the duration of the ceremony, and when the ceremony has finished, they are freshly laundered and once again housed in the altar, to await the next divine manifestation. Once the *lwa* departs, the 'horse' is left exhausted, with no memory of what has transpired during the trance state.

Ceremonies typically begin with participants wearing crisp, dazzlingly white garments, a symbol of purity and cleanliness, contrasting starkly with both the dark skin of the wearers and the red blood of any animal that may have been sacrificed. In Haiti, where both Maya Deren (1970 [1953]) in the early 1940s and Susan Tselos (2000) in the 1990s observed Vodou ceremonies, the men wore white cotton shirts over white cotton trousers and the women wore white dresses of varying designs but with full skirts reaching to below the knees and wide sleeves, both outfits allowed for ease of movement. Women's heads were encased in a white *mouchoir* (kerchief). When dancing, the women would hold the hems of their dresses, revealing a flurry of white petticoats; the men would hold either end of a scarf that was draped around their necks. As well as the traditional textiles and material goods that formed part of Vodou's African roots, more modern embellishments have been added in the form of sequins, buttons and other decorative elements not widely available in Africa (Deren 1970 [1953]; Tselos 2000).

If a ceremony is to honour and pay respect to a particular *lwa*, the colours associated with that *lwa* are evident. Colours are recognized for their quality of coolness or warmth: the Yoruba term *funfun* refers to white, silver and grey, colours said to evoke coolness and that are associated with age and wisdom; *pupa* which denotes warm or hot is represented by red, orange, deep yellow and pink, associated with passion and aggression; and *dudu* which bridges the hot/warm and cold/cool categories and incorporates dark colours such as black, blue, purple and green, dark brown, dark red and dark grey (Tselos 2000:48).

Temperaments, personality and heat or coolness are linked and form part of the system of correspondences associated with particular *lwa*. The colours that represent the *lwa* are seen not only in the garments worn during possession but also in the garments worn by *serviteurs* (those who serve the *lwa*) to protect themselves from evil and to attract good energy to themselves. The *lwa* and humans have a reciprocal association. Vodou followers look after the *lwa* by pleasing them, and in turn, they are protected by the *lwa*; those who have been initiated are bestowed with certain powers and psychic abilities. It is said that the *lwa* depend on the rites performed for them for their sustenance and that without these rites, they would wither and die, an interesting notion that gives great depth to the psychology that is built into these religions.

In order to prepare the way for the *lwa* to be attracted to a Haitian Vodou ritual, intricate lace-like designs, called *vévé*, specific to each *lwa*, are traced out on the ground with flour or ground coffee. In these designs, vertical lines represent the spirit; horizontal lines represent matter, and when they transverse, the meeting point that forms a cross represents the meeting of spirit and matter. As well, there is a pole (*poteau-mitan*), reaching from ceiling to floor in the centre of the ceremonial space, that links the spiritual realm with the physical realm, allowing the *lwa* a portal through which to enter the realm of humans (Deren 1970 [1953]:36).

Some of the major *lwa* of the Vodou pantheon are Papa Legba, Gédé, Baron Samdi, Dambala and Ezili. Each one is associated with a specific element of nature (earth, air, fire, water), tree or plant, human behaviour, and colour. Papa Legba is the first *lwa* to be invoked as he 'opens the gate' that separates humans from the supernatural world, allowing other *lwa* to enter the ceremonial sacred space. In Haiti, Legba shares the attributes of the Christian saint Peter, who holds the keys to heaven. Other *lwa* also have their Roman Catholic counterparts in the saints; for example, Ezili corresponds with the Virgin Mary and Dambala with St Patrick. Some of Legba's correspondences are the colours red and white, the calabash tree and the realm of earth, and his symbol is a feeble old man in rags.

The circle is the symbol of the powerful Dambala, the *lwa* associated with snakes. Dambala's correspondences are the colour white, all food that is white, the principle of goodness, springs, rivers, water and the snake-rainbow. Someone possessed of Dambala dances in snake-like movements or writhes and undulates sinuously on the temple floor, representing Dambala as a great snake undergirding and encircling the world, whose coiling movements trace the path of the sun and the rotation of the earth and stars. A necklace of blue and white trade beads interspersed with snake vertebrae represents Dambala, along with such items as a pair of white roosters, Florida Water, barley water, sugar cookies and eggs, as well as various herbs, roots and powders.

Baron Samdi, also called Baron Cimetière or Baron La Croix, is the leader of the Gédé, a family of graveyard spirits who act as guardians of the dead and intermediaries between life and death. As the Gédé are strongly associated with death, their symbols are cadavers and crosses; their colours are black, purple and white; and animal correspondences are primarily goats and cocks. Subterranean places and cemeteries are linked with the Gédé. One *lwa* is called Gédé Nibo, an assistant gravedigger who frequents graveyards. Celebrants honouring Baron Samdi dress in purple and black, often with a black top hat, cut-away jackets, black-and-white striped pants and a white shirt with a handkerchief in the pocket. They tend to wear sunglasses and have their faces powdered white. Baron Samdi is invariably depicted as a skeleton dressed in black. As well as being influenced by Catholicism, there are numerous Masonic Lodges in Haiti, and Freemasonry symbols are present at funerals and as part of the symbols of the Gédé (Tselos 2000:55).

Ezili, like the other *lwa*, has different facets or personalities. As Ezili Freda, she is the goddess of feminine beauty, love and grace, the epitome of charm, and usually displays either coquettish and flirtatious behaviour or provocative and seductive behaviour. Curiously, her Catholic counterpart is the Virgin Mary. Her colours are pale blue and pink, and she is associated with riverbanks and water; her symbols are the heart and a mirror. Ezili likes to be offered gifts of perfume, combs, brushes, mirrors, jewellery, soaps and flowers. During possession by Ezili, the 'horse' is dressed in fine lace, satin, gold jewels, pearls and perfumes. Many men become 'married' to Ezili Freda, building a bedroom for her and decorating it in white, with drapes of lace, and spraying it with perfume. A man who marries Ezili pledges to 'sleep' with her every Thursday night and to abstain from sexual intercourse with others on that day.

The *lwa* are dedicated to serving humans, but they will not bestow their largesse until they are welcomed and well fed. A very specific protocol must be followed before they appear. Possession, initiation and mystical marriage are special forms of close contact with the *lwa*. The experience of possession by a *lwa* indicates that the spirit is calling the devotee to its service. Their heads must be washed to open them to the *lwa* without impurities or resistance, to become true *serviteurs* of the *lwa*, or to become prepared for a spiritual marriage with a particular *lwa*. Such preparation may include special clothes, food, liquors and lotions, such as a new nightdress, a new ceremonial dress, a necklace. Initiation includes the *lave-tet*, washing of the head with infusions of herbs and medicinal plants, and a strict diet. Initiates are dressed in white, with a white kerchief knotted around the head, which has been covered for the duration of the confinement with a poultice made of medicinal herbs and foods. The clothes worn by the initiates are made specifically for them to be worn only during ceremony or other religious events. Occasionally, the white garments might have material from white lace tablecloths and napkins added (Tselos 2000:59). Much time, care and attention is given to the making of the garments.

If a person is possessed by a *lwa* during the ceremony it indicates that that person is forever linked with that spirit until death; in turn, the *lwa* bestows mystical powers and psychic abilities on the person.

SANTERÍA

The Santería[3] religion of Latin America has its origins among the Yoruba priests and priestesses of Nigeria who, during the end of the eighteenth and the first few decades of the nineteenth centuries, were among those Africans transported into slavery to the Americas (Bodin 1990). The name Santería derives from the Spanish Catholic term *santos*, or saint, which became equated with the Yoruba term *orisha* when the Yoruba religion merged Catholic saints with their traditional African spirits. Santería is similar to Haitian Vodou with its mixture of animism, pantheism, ancestor worship and Catholicism. The central belief is that everything in the universe is made of a cosmic energy whose source is God the Creator. The *orishas* are messengers and repositories of God's energy. Sacrificial blood represents the energy from which all things are created; it is living energy from which the spiritual world is both formed and nourished. To offer blood, therefore, is to offer the *orisha* the gift of energy.

Figure 7.1   Santería high priest, Havana, Cuba. Photo: Getty Images.

During the first of many initiations, an initiate receives five *collares*, or bead necklaces, each one consecrated to one of the major saints/*orishas*: Obatalá, Changó, Yemayá, Oshún and Oyá, who with Eleggua are the foundation of Santería. Obatalá dresses in white because he is very pure—the patron of peace and purity; he is also the father of the *orishas* but is nevertheless equated with the Catholic Our Lady of Mercy. Changó, associated with the colours red and white, is the patron of fire, thunder and lightning, victory over both enemies and adversities, and is equated with St Barbara. Yemayá, whose colour is blue, is the patron of the seas and motherhood and is equally viewed as Our Lady of Regla. Oshún, also known as Our Lady of La Caridad del Cobre, patron saint of Cuba, is the patron of love and marriage; her colours are red and yellow (González-Wippler 1992).

Santería's equivalent of the Vodoun *Iwa* Legba is Eleggua, the most important of the *orishas* because he must be addressed first in order to call in anyone else. He is the guardian of the doors and the crossroads and without his good will, the other *orishas* can do nothing. The *orishas* incorporate everything that exists; every stone, bird, flower, tree, and fruit and all natural phenomena such as rainbows, clouds and rain, as well as every human thought, action and enterprise. The *orishas* are the focus of all worship, and Santería practitioners become involved in a reciprocal arrangement with a particular *orisha* (González-Wippler 1992:26, 305).

Each of the major *orishas* have various aspects that manifest in a slightly different manner. For example the generic Yemayá might appear in seven separate guises or paths. The oldest and most important is Yemayá Awoyo, who wears seven skirts to fight for her children and crowns herself with the rainbow. The wise and haughty Yemayá Ayawa wears a silver anklet and listens to her children only with her back toward them. The warrior aspect of Yemayá is Yemayá Okuti who can be violent and does not forget an offense; when she fights she carries a knife and other weapons hanging from her belt. As Yemayá Konla, she lives in the sea foam; Yemayá Mayalewo lives in the forests in a saltwater pool where she works her most powerful spells, while Yemayá Asesu lives in the sewers and other unclean waters (González-Wippler 1992).

All participants come to Santería ceremonies well scrubbed and wearing immaculate white garments: males wear white cotton trousers, sweaters or shirts, and are barefoot, or in sneakers; females wear wide white cotton skirts and ruffled petticoats that swirl and swish as their dancing gets underway. Cleanliness and purity are equated, and white is considered to be the most pure colour. It is therefore the colour most evident during Santería ceremonies, with the addition of the specific colours associated with each *orisha*.

A ritual cannot proceed without the accompaniment of drumming and trance dancing, a quintessential part of any ceremony of the religions of the African diaspora. The drums and the singing excite all those who attend and help to call down the *orishas*. The dancers sway and move with shuffled feet to the beats of the drumming. At different times during a ceremony, the drumbeat changes tempo, increasing when an impassioned call heralds the invocation of an *orisha*, and the dancing becomes faster paced.

Although most of the dancing is done by stamping the feet to the drumbeat and shuffling back and forth, the upper body movements usually indicate which *orisha* is being 'danced'. Male *orishas* tend to be more violent in their motions; Changó for example stomps up and down with his fists clenched in front of his chest like a boxer. Female *orishas*, on the other hand, like to swing their skirts with their hands in rhythm with the drumbeat, and each beats her skirt in a different way; Yemayá undulates like the sea waves, while Oyá, who pertains to the cemetery, waves one hand in the air as she fans her skirt with the other, and an *orisha* called Olocun loves to dance with a snake wrapped around her rider's body. The enculturated audience knows from these signs which *orisha* is present (González-Wippler 1992:213).

When Oshún enters into a rider's body, the person takes on a flirtatious manner. Wrapping him- or herself in a yellow silk mantle the rider swings the fringes of the mantle in a saucy, teasing way, fanning the air with the five handkerchiefs associated with Oshún, perhaps singing a love song and moving in a seductive way, jingling five gold bracelets as he or she moves. This behaviour becomes apparent even if Oshún occupies a male body.

The *orisha* Babalú was an old beggar during his life on earth, so he wears knee-length sackcloth pants and shuffles like a weary old man, but the sackcloth is trimmed with purple, his preferred color, and gold designs are added to the sleeves and legs. The colour purple follows through into flowers, his favourites being irises, orchids, lavender and other purple-hued blossoms. Purple silk handkerchiefs embroidered in gold are also associated with Babalú, who has a wide purple band around his temples as well as two purple shoulder bags criss-crossed across his chest. Bare-legged and barefoot, he carries a large sheaf of herbs tied with a purple ribbon on his right hand and a long staff on his left (González-Wippler 1992).

The term *asiento* refers to a process of initiation that culminates in the *orisha*'s possession of the initiate's body, and a reciprocal pact is made between the living person and the *orisha*. This initiation is called *hacer santo* which means to 'make the saint'. When this is successful, it is believed that the person is given all of the saint's supernatural powers. On becoming an *asiento* (male) or *asienta* (female), the person must not look in a mirror for three months and must keep the head covered the whole time. Women are forbidden facial make-up, depilation, eyebrow plucking and curling or colouring their hair. They must be dressed in white for a year, with a white handkerchief wrapped around their heads. The necklaces and bracelets of the *orishas* are the only jewellery permitted. Having undergone these strict rules however the benefits are apparently great: the *orisha* answers all their questions and advises them, and they gain knowledge of spiritual things, herbal cures and spells, and certain 'powers' or psychic abilities such as clairvoyance, the gift of healing and prophecy (González-Wippler 1992:200).

At one *asiento* ceremony described by González-Wippler (1992:284), a woman who had been possessed by Obatalá wore

> a beautiful gown made of white *peau de soie* embroidered in tiny pearls, with a wide skirt, fluffy sleeves, and a high neckline. A wide crown, made of the same materials as her dress, completely encircled her forehead, covering her shaved head, she wore the *collar de mazo*, the necklaces, and the bracelets, of the orishas: seven silver for Yemayá, five golden for Oshún, nine copper for Oyá, and a solitary silver one for Obatalá, her orisha. The walls and ceiling over her were draped with white lace and silver brocade. There were white flowers all around her, and she looked breathtakingly beautiful. As she stood by her 'throne', she was no longer a woman, but Obatalá himself in all his unearthly beauty.

For three months after the ceremony, restrictions were placed on the woman's behaviour and activities. When the three months were over, there were more ritual cleanings and chants. For the obligatory one year of her initiation course, she was dressed in meticulous white, her head modestly covered by a white handkerchief, tied African style. She had to wear her necklaces and bracelets at all times, except during her menstruation. Finally, at the end of the initiation year, she was given the *libreta* (book of secrets), her coronation clothes, and the hair that had been cut from her head during the *asiento*. This hair would be placed in her coffin upon her death, and the dress and other fineries would be worn for her final 'voyage'.

Migene González-Wippler was raised in the Santería faith from a young age and her personal journey with the Santería ceremonies provides us with much firsthand information. When she was only seven years of age, she was taken to a ceremony that was intended to thank the *orisha* Changó, the spirit of lightning and thunder, for granting a favour to one of his followers. Changó's colours are red and white, so congregants dressed in these colours to honour him. She describes her own dress for this occasion:

> I was dressed in a swirling white dress and spotless white sandals. Around my head was a white handkerchief tied with a knot in front, African style. Around my throat was a necklace of alternating white and red beads. I swung my body around, and the wide skirt billowed gracefully around me. (1992:39)

The adult woman who took her to the ceremony wore a white cotton skirt, a dazzlingly white petticoat trimmed with yards of ruffled cotton lace underneath, a white handkerchief on her head and many coloured bead necklaces shining over the pleated skirt front, which, writes González-Wippler, 'contrasted agreeably with her dark skin' (1992:39). Another elderly woman who was offering the ceremony to Changó was splendidly attired in bright red taffeta trimmed with white lace that no doubt rustled as she moved, and on her head she wore a red handkerchief adorned with four brightly coloured feathers; coloured beads covered her neck, wrists and ankles.

González-Wippler details what happens during a ceremony when an invocation to an *orisha* occurs and the *orisha* is thought to descend to 'mount' its 'rider'. In the invocation to Changó, she recalls how impassioned the dancing became. At one point, a tall, barefooted and bareheaded man, dressed in white with a red sash tied around his waist, began to sway heavily from side to side. He lost his balance and when he stumbled clumsily into the centre of the circle people began to shout: 'Give way! Changó's here! Changó's here!' The *orisha* Changó had possessed the man's body.

At this, she recalls, the drums increased their intensity, people fell back from the centre of the circle where the tall man spun faster and faster, his body shaking uncontrollably, his mouth lax, his eyes rolling. After moving in this way for some time, he stopped suddenly, straightening his body with an obvious effort. His eyes were open but unfocused, and he kept working his mouth from side to side in 'a terrible grimace', a frightening sight and an unforgettable experience for a seven-year-old girl who was witnessing a Santería ceremony for the first time, especially when the man grabbed two double-edged steel axes and began to swing them wildly around his head while continuing to dance.

In the dimly candle-lit room, he looked, she remarked, 'awesomely powerful, his body rippling with superhuman strength'. This mere mortal had been completely transformed. Changó had indeed arrived. Just as suddenly however, the ritual dance stopped; the drums fell silent, and Changó, now in total possession of the man, turned to survey his audience. Once Changó had relayed messages to certain members of the audience, the *orisha* was ready to leave; the man began to shake convulsively and he was left in a comatose-like slump, his body bathed in sweat.

CANDOMBLÉ

A variety of African religious traditions that were established in Brazil in the nineteenth century appear under the generic term Candomblé. Devotees refer to group actions in honour of the spirits (*orixás*) as 'making Candomblé'. Like Vodou and Santería, possession by spirits is paramount in Candomblé ceremonies.[4] The *orixás* are called upon to help the living and the devotees in turn dedicate themselves to the *orixás*. Each *orixá* has several different personalities, each with its own likes and dislikes, preferences for objects, food and dress, and is readily recognized when it appears in its human vessel. The success of any ceremony also depends upon the success of how well the food was prepared as well as the vast repertoire of secret prayers that accompany the food's preparation, all of which combine to tempt the *orixás* to attend the feast and to enter a human body.

An important Candomblé ceremony that is long and costly is one that prepares a person to be a 'bride' of the spirit, known as *iaô*. In order for this to occur, the devotee must first have been 'called' by the *orixá*, something which is made dramatically clear, usually by a spontaneous manifestation of a spirit at a ceremony, when the *orixá* enters, unbidden, into the consciousness and body of an untrained person. Once this happens, it is inevitable that the devotee becomes a 'bride' and that she devotes the rest of her life to the service of her particular *orixá* (Murphy 1994).

To become a bride, the individual must go through a lengthy initiation that can last months, in order to fully immerse herself into the life of service to the *orixá*, and to bring the presence of the *orixá* into her life and those around her. A shrine is established with materials on it that correspond to the specific *orixá*, such as a stone and emblems that become imbued with the presence of the *orixá* over time. Initiation into Candomblé then firmly establishes the *orixá*'s presence into the consciousness of the initiate (known as the *abian*) (Murphy 1994).

The first part of this lengthy initiation is the cutting of the *abian*'s hair. Seated in a pure white, strapless dress that is elasticized at the bust one senior priestess cuts her hair as closely as possible to the scalp, while another senior priestess holds a lighted white candle. The spirit is invoked by sounds and smells: the sound of a metal bell being rung and both priestesses chanting songs appropriate to the *orixá* and the aroma of an herbal infusion used to bathe the *abian*'s head.

The head is extremely important and needs to be treated with utmost respect and reverence, as the centre of the head is regarded as the seat of consciousness, the point of intersection between the spirit realm and the human world, and is the medium for the presence of the *orixás*. Bracelets, armlets and anklets that have been bathed in the same herbal liquid are given to each *abian* as well as a heavy necklace of coloured beads that correspond to the colours of the *orixá* (Murphy 1994:60).

Figure 7.2 Candomblé priestess in Bahia, Brazil. Photo: Getty Images.

Beads are, in fact, an essential part of Candomblé's sacred dress. Once Candomblé beads were worn only by Candomblé initiates. Over time uninitiated people began to wear the beads as a signifier of cultural identity, a personal display of their African-ness as well as for protection and good luck. Consecrated beads, however, are special. When beads are consecrated by sacred herbs or blood from a sacrificial offering, they are considered to be imbued with powerful forces from the *orixá* themselves. Touching or wearing such beads transfers the essence of the *orixá* to the wearer, linking them to the spiritual force of the *orixá*. Thus, the beads become divine in themselves (Shirey 2012:36). Beads are usually made out of glass, plastic or clay, and the colour, shape, size and position of the beads can be 'read' for meanings by the culturally attuned viewer. Because beads are worn so close to the head, that part of the body considered to be where the spiritual force of the *orixá* resides and the origin of one's own spirit, they are more important as necklaces. For those who wear them for sacred purposes rather than for secular reasons, they might be hidden from public view under a garment to avoid revealing sacred information and their affiliation with the religion as well as prevent ostracism or persecution from evangelical Christians in the wider community (Shirey 2012:48).

During the long months that follow this initial ceremony, the *abian* becomes progressively more open to the world of the spirits, until eventually, an *orixá*

Figure 7.3   Three young women in a Candomblé ritual, Bahia, Brazil. Photo: Getty Images.

speaks through the *abian*. In preparation for this to happen, the presiding priestesses set out candles and drape the *abians* in white cloth in honour of the foundation *orixá*, Oxala. Again, the head is the focal point and is once more washed in the herbal infusions and shaved. A bell is rung vigorously and the *orixá*, speaking through the *abian*, is identified.

The *abians* are then ready to be presented publicly to the rest of the community, to the accompaniment of drums, dances and songs. The head of the *abian* is painted with a white chalky paste, giving it a luminous appearance, to herald the presence of Oxala, the most senior *orixá*, whose presence is necessary in order for any of the other *orixás* to come through. Now, with the *orixá* firmly within the body and consciousness of the *abian*, the first offering is ready to be received. Each *abian* holds a small white bird in her hand while the priestesses invoke the *orixá* within. The bird is subsequently strangled, and its blood poured over the consecrated head of the *abian*, who sits in the dripping life-blood that is so essential for the *orixá*'s continuing strength; the bird's feathers are plucked and stuck to the drying blood (Murphy 1994:61–2).

A third and final 'intensification of the head' then occurs, this time through the form of an incision in the centre of the scalp. A cross is cut which literally opens a point of intersection between inner and outer worlds, spirit and human. A thick poultice of the same herbs used previously is rubbed into the cut, 'inoculating' initiates with the power of their *orixás*. Their arms and shoulders are also incised, and they are henceforth considered true brides of their *orixás*.

Another festive ceremony for the newly made brides includes the brides coming out to the community three times, each time dressed in different garb, heralded by different drum rhythms. The first time they are dressed in white skirts to represent the creativity of the male *orixá,* Oxala, and their heads are painted with a single red parrot feather tied around the forehead, the red to represent the female spirit Oxun. At the second coming out, they are dressed in the colours of their specific *orixás* and in skirts with voluminous petticoats.

For their third and final appearance, the brides are dressed in the complete regalia of their specific *orixás*. For example:

Iansá dances in pink taffeta, her head surmounted by a high-peaked, studded pink crown with short lines of beads covering her face. She carries a bouquet of long lilies in her right hand and a short, ornamental copper sword in her left. Iemanjá wears white. Her crown is smaller and clear beads shield her face. Her bouquet of lilies is tied with a blue ribbon, and she holds the *abébé*, the white metal mirror and fan of a great lady. Omulu's costume is the most dramatic of all.

His head is covered in the *iko*, a great cone of dried raffia, golden palm straw from Africa. His skirt is also of raffia. In his hand he carries the *xaxara*, a short ornamental broom which sweeps the *terreiro* [building and grounds] free of disease and death. (Murphy 1994:63)

The feelings of being taken over by an *orixá* are described by one senior priestess as follows:

my legs tremble, something reaches up that takes over my heart, my head grows, I see that blue light, I look for someone to grab but can't find anyone and then I don't see anything anymore. Then everything happens and I don't see. Then I think the Orisha (*orixá*) must be something like a wind, it comes toward you like a wind and embraces you. Like a shock in my heart, my heart beats as fast as the lead drum plays, my head grows, and it seems like I see a blue light ahead of me and a hole appears in the middle of the room. Then I want to run, to grab someone, but people seem far away, out of reach. Then I don't see anything any more. (Murphy 1994:61)

At this point, the devotee has entered a trance state and has 'become' the *orixá*.

As can be seen, there are very strong similarities with the three major branches of the African diaspora. There is the experience of possession by the spirit, the devotee is called to its service, the head is the focal point of consciousness and the entry of the spirits. In Vodou, like the Candomblé 'bride', the head of the *serviteur* needs to be made pure in order to open the person up to the entry of the spirits, and the spiritual marriage with a particular *lwa* includes special clothes, food, liquors and lotions, such as a new nightdress, a new ceremonial dress, and a necklace, in the case of the Vodoun Dambala.

Each of the spirits in all three sections of the African diaspora has a different set of facets, or personalities, that require specific items from their *serviteurs* that are appropriate. Each spirit has particular likes and dislikes, dress requirements, foods, chants, drum rhythms, needs and desires, and even dance movements and very specific gestures, as relayed here by Murphy (1994:70), citing Edison Carneiro:

Suppose that you are dancing for Oxossi, the hunter. Touch your right forefinger to your left thumb and, besides these, let only your left little finger be extended. Shimmy your shoulders. Shake your arms, but keep your shoulders still. Keep your buttocks turned out. Your feet dance in the same tramp-tramp, but the upper parts of your body move in different rhythms, depending upon the drums. Now, flop your body down from the waist, and sweep it languorously from one side to another. Twist your pelvis around.

To merely write about all these ceremonies does not fully convey the atmosphere of excitement, joy and reverence, the visual éclat of swaying full petticoats, the loud insistent, vigorous drumming, the evocative chanting, the visuals of people going into a full trance and metamorphosing into a spirit, their consciousness having been completely taken over by spirit, the gestures of supplication by participants, and the smells of sweat, food, animals and blood. Murphy comes close to allowing us glimpses:

> The appearance of the orixás is like a burst of light, dazzling and multifaceted, into the *barracão* [dance court]. The polished crowns and instruments, and bright silk and satins of the garments, augmented by the rhythmic propulsions of the drums startle the senses to appreciate the epiphany of the orixás among the congregation. (1994:73)

In the three religions that have been covered very briefly here, Vodou, Santería and Candomblé, the spirit as the 'rider' works through a particular person as its 'horse' for the benefit, instruction and assistance of both individuals and community. Both rider and horse have reciprocal obligations to each other. The entire community is also responsible for this reciprocal arrangement because everyone benefits, and without human participation, it is said, the spirits themselves would cease to exist.

The vibrant dress, dance, drums and songs all contribute to the sensual performance of every ceremony, with each spirit displaying archetypal identities that all participants can relate to and with, not only during the ceremony, but in their daily lives. The link between human and spirit is played out with energy, a deep understanding of the human psyche and the uplifting of a people in the face of enormous adversity.

Notes

CHAPTER 1 HIERARCHIES AND POWER

1. Material for this chapter primarily draws from those authors cited, as well as *The Catholic Encyclopedia* (www.newadvent.org/cathen); Dwyer (1995); Kay and Rubin (1994); and Kuhns (2003).
2. Colours of vestments can also change according to the Church's calendar of events and the seasons of the year. Refer in the first instance to *The Catholic Encyclopedia* online (www.newadvent.org/cathen). We are concerned here principally with how vestments relate to rank.
3. Personal communication with Sisters of Mercy nuns, Brisbane, Australia, 2004.
4. Ibid.
5. Ibid.
6. Ibid.
7. Linda Arthur (personal communication) suggests that the Mother Hubbard dress might have stemmed from the Hawaiian Holoku, about which she has written (see Arthur 1998), and that further research on the Mother Hubbard dress and its origins is forthcoming.
8. The author lived in Noumea, New Caledonia, for three years, from 1969 to 1972, and observed at first-hand women wearing these dresses on a daily basis, including while they played cricket, another introduced cultural item; both continue to exist.
9. Information for Yoruba is from Renne (2000).
10. Information from author's unpublished PhD thesis (Hume 1990).
11. Information for this section from Taylor (2009) and Litten (1991).

CHAPTER 2 SIMPLICITY AND HUMILITY

1. Sources for background information on the Anabaptists in addition to those texts cited: *The Canadian Encyclopedia* (www.thecanadianencyclopedia.com); *The Catholic Encyclopedia* (www.newadvent.org/cathen/10190b.htm); Swatos (1998); Melton and Baumann (2002); www.hutteriteheritage.com; www.history. mennonite.net/; and www.hutterites.org/religion.htm

2. The author visited Hutterite communities in Alberta, Canada, during her fifteen years living in Alberta (1977–1992), after having met some Hutterite women during their stay in a Calgary hospital.
3. See www.hutteriteheritage.com
4. Ibid.
5. Ibid.
6. Ibid.
7. See Hurst and McConnell (2010) for the complex nuances of everyday Amish life and how they deal with changes that are forced on them from the outside.
8. The Young Center for Anabaptist and Pietist Studies, Elizabethtown College, 'Amish Population Trends 2008–2013, Five-Year Highlights' (www2.etown.edu/amishstudies/Population_Trends_2012.asp).

CHAPTER 3 FASHIONING FAITH

1. Sources for background information on Judaism in addition to those cited in text: *Encyclopedia Britannica* (2003); Neusner, Avery Peck and Green (2000); Landman (2009); Cohn-Sherbok (1998); Maher (2006); www.jewfaq.org/signs. htm; and www.jewishvirtuallibrary.org/jsource/Judaism/Kippah.html
2. Sources for background information on Islam in addition to those texts cited: *Encyclopedia Britannica* (2003); Melton and Baumann (2002); Smart (1989); and Khuri (2001).
3. See www.jewfaq.org/signs.htm
4. Ibid.
5. Ibid.

CHAPTER 4 INDIA

1. The author spent time in India in 2006.
2. Banerjee and Miller (2003) provided a substantial amount of information for the section on the sari, as well as Shukla (2008). See also Kawlra (2010), Maynard (2004) and http://utopia.knoware.nl/users/dolfhart/sects.html for background information on dress and globalization.
3. The author visited some textile shops on a tour of India in 2006.
4. Some background sources for information on Hindus: Flood (1996); Melton and Baumann (2010); www.bbc.co.uk/religion/religions/hinduism/
5. See Hullet and Roces (1981); www.geovision.com.my/malaysia/general/religious/festivals/thaipusam.html

6. Sources for background information on Sadhus: Flood (1996); Hartsuiker (1993); Hausner (2007); http://utopia.knoware.nl.users/olfhart/sects.html
7. See http://utopia.knoware.nl.users/olfhart/sects.html
8. Sources for background information on Sikhs: N.-G. Singh (2004); Melton and Baumann(2002);McLeod(1989);www.sikhs.org/;www.sikhnet.com/s/WhyTurbans; www.bbc.co.uk/religion/religions/sikhism/customs/fiveks.shtml
9. See www.bbc.co.uk/religion/religions/sikhism/customs/fiveks.shtml
10. See www.sikhnet.com/s/WhyTurbans
11. Sources for background information on Jains: Vallely (2009); Cort (2001); www.bbc.co.uk/religion/religions/jainism; www.jainism.org; www.bbc.co.uk/religion/religions/jainism/; www.dlshq.org/religions/jainism.htm
12. See www.ahimsasilks.com/

CHAPTER 5 THE BUDDHA, THE DHARMA, THE SANGHA . . . AND THE ROBE

1. Sources for background information on Buddhism: *Encyclopedia Britannica* (2003); *Oxford Dictionary of Buddhism* (2004); Andersen (1979); Batchelor (2010); Beer (2004); Buswell (2003); Karuna (2012); Tanabe (2003); Thurman (1995); Bikku (1998); www.buddhanet/pdf_file/bhkkrule.pdf); Sopa (2007/2008); www.BuddhaNet.net.
2. Interviewed by Lynne Hume at Chenrezig Buddhist community, Queensland, Australia in June 2012.
3. Evans-Wentz (1973); Kramer (1988); *Encyclopedia Britannica* (2003).

CHAPTER 6 SUFIS, INDIGENOUS SHAMANS AND MODERN PAGANS

1. Sources for background information on the Sufis: Bearman et al. (2009); Corbin (1969); Ernst and Lawrence (2002); Helminksi (2006); Netton (2000); www.sufism.org/society/sema2.html; www.whirlingdervishes.org/whirlingdervishes.htm
2. Sources for background information on Shamanism: Czaplicka (1914); Kendall (1985); Kister (2004); Lommel (1967); Potapov (1999); Townsend (1997); Vitebsky (2001); Walter and Fridman (2004).
3. The author carried out research on modern Paganism in 1991 (in Canada and the United States) and 1992–2000 (in Australia). Much of the information is gleaned from this research. See Hume (1997). See also Valiente (1978); Ezzy (2011); and Pike (2001).

CHAPTER 7 POSSESSION

1. The practice of blood sacrifice no longer occurs everywhere.
2. Sources for background information on Vodou: Bodin (1990); Brown (1991); Deren (1970 [1953]); Gordon (2000); Hurbon (1995); and Tselos (2000).
3. Sources for Santería drawn principally from González-Wippler (1992); Murphy (1994); and Gordon (2000). See also De La Torre (2004) and Pérez y Mena (1998, 1999).
4. Sources for Candomblé: Murphy (1994); Shirey (2012); Wafer (1991); www.bbc. co.uk/religion/religions/candomble/.

Bibliography

Aherne, M. C. (1983), *Joyous Service: The History of the Sisters of Saint Joseph of Springfield,* Holyoke: Sisters of Saint Joseph.

Anderson, W. (1979), *Open Secrets: A Western Guide to Tibetan Buddhism*, New York: Viking Press.

Arthur, L. B. (1998), 'Fossilized Fashion in Hawai'i', *Paideusis: Journal for Interdisciplinary and Cross-Cultural Studies,* 1:15–28.

Arthur, L. B. (1999), 'Dress and the Social Control of the Body', in L. Arthur (ed.), *Religion, Dress and the Body*, Oxford: Berg, pp. 1–8.

Arthur, L. B. (2004), 'Clothing: Dress and Religion in America's Sectarian Communities', in L. Jones (ed.), *Encyclopedia of Religion,* 2nd ed., vol. 3, Detroit, MI: Macmillan, pp. 1834–7.

Banerjee, M., and Miller, D. (2003), *The Sari*, Oxford: Berg.

Bank, R. D. (2005), *Judaism: Beliefs, Practices, Customs and Traditions*, Avon, MA: Adams Media.

Batchelor, M. (2005), 'Nuns: Buddhist Nuns', in L. Jones (ed.), *Encyclopedia of Religion,* 2nd ed., vol. 10, Detroit, MI: Macmillan Reference, Gale Virtual Reference Library, pp. 6759–63.

Batchelor, M. (2010), *The Spirit of the Buddha,* New Haven, CT: Yale University Press.

Batra, S. (1999), *The Art of Mehndi*, New York: Penguin.

Bearman, P., Bianquis, Th., Bosworth, C. E., van Donzel, E., and Heinrichs, W. P. (eds) (2009), *Encyclopaedia of Islam,* Leiden: Brill.

Beer, R. (2004), *The Encyclopedia of Tibetan Symbols and Motifs*, Boston: Shambhala Publications.

Berger, P. L. (1970), *A Rumour of Angels: Modern Society and the Rediscovery of the Supernatural*, London: Allen Lane.

Berndt, R. M., and Berndt, C. H. (1977), *The World of the First Australians*, Sydney: Ure Smith.

Bikku, A. (1998), *The Bikkhu's Rules: A Guide for Laypeople,* Kallista, Australia: Sanghaleka Forest Heritage.

Bodin, R. (1990), *Voodoo: Past and Present,* Lafayette: The Center for Louisiana Studies, University of Southwestern Louisiana.

Bourdieu, P. (1973), 'Cultural Reproduction and Social Reproduction', in R. Brown (ed.), *Knowledge, Education and Social Change*, London: Tavistock, pp. 71–112.

Brown, K. (1991), *Mama Lola: A Voudou Priestess in Brooklyn,* Berkeley: University of California Press.

Buswell, R. E. Jr. (2003), *Encyclopedia of Buddhism,* New York: Macmillan Reference.

Bynum, C. W. (1987), *Holy Feast and Holy Fast: The Religious Significance of Food to Medieval Women*, Berkeley: University of California Press.

Bynum, C. W. (1991), *Fragmentation and Redemption: Essays on Gender and the Human Body in Medieval Religion*, New York: Zone Books.

Carrel, B. G. (1999), 'Hasidic Women's Head Coverings: A Feminized System of Hasidic Distinction', in L. Arthur (ed.), *Religion, Dress and the Body*, Oxford: Berg, pp. 31–52.

Classen, C. (2005), *The Book of Touch*, Oxford: Berg.

Classen, C. (2012), *The Deepest Sense: A Cultural History of Touch*, Champaign: University of Illinois Press.

Classen, C., Howes, D., and Synnott, A. (1994), *Aroma: The Cultural History of Smell*, London: Routledge.

Cohn-Sherbok, D. (1998), *A Concise Encyclopedia of Judaism,* Oxford: One World Publications.

Comaroff, J. (1985), *Body of Power, Spirit of Resistance: The Culture and History of a South African People*, Chicago: University of Chicago Press.

Corbin, H. (1969), *Creative Imagination in the Sufism of Ibn 'Arabi,* trans. R. Manheim, Princeton, NJ: Princeton University Press.

Cort, J. E. (2001), *Jains in the World: Religious Values and Ideology in India,* New York: Oxford University Press.

Czaplicka, M. A. (1914), 'Shamanism in Siberia', *Internet Sacred Text Archive*, chap. 10, www.sacred-texts.com, accessed 10 January 2012.

Daly, C. M. (1999), 'The "Paarda" Expression of Hejaab among Afghan Women in a Non-Muslim Community', in L. B. Arthur (ed.), *Religion, Dress and the Body*, Oxford: Berg, pp. 147–61.

Daly, C. M. (2000), 'The Afghan Woman's "Chaadaree": An Evocative Religious Expression?', in L. B. Arthur (ed.), *Undressing Religion: Commitment and Conversion from a Cross-Cultural Perspective*, Oxford: Berg, pp. 131–46.

Davis, F. (1992), *Fashion, Culture and Identity*, Chicago: University of Chicago Press.

De La Torre, M. (2004), *Santería: The Beliefs and Rituals of a Growing Religion in America,* Grand Rapids, MI: Wm. B. Eerdmans Publishing.

Deren, M. (1970 [1953]), *Divine Horsemen: The Living Gods of Haiti*, New York: McPherson and Company.

Douglas, M. (1982), *Natural Symbols*, New York: Pantheon Books.

Druesedow, J. L. (2010), 'Snapshot: Amish, Mennonites, Hutterites, and Brethren', in J. B. Eicher (ed.), *Berg Encyclopedia of World Dress and Fashion*, vol. 3, Oxford: Berg, pp. 496–8.

Dupree, L. (1980), *Afghanistan*, Princeton, NJ: Princeton University Press.

Durkheim, E. (1915), *The Elementary Forms of the Religious Life*, trans. Joseph Ward Swain, London: Allen and Unwin.

Dwyer, E. J. (1995), *Vestments,* Sydney: Catholic Press.

Ebaugh, H. (1977), *Out of the Cloister: A Study of Organizational Dilemmas*, Austin: University of Texas Press.

Eck, D. L. (1998), *Darśan: Seeing the Divine Image in India*, 3rd ed., New York: Columbia University Press.

Eicher, J. B. (2010), 'Introduction to Global Perspectives', in J. B. Eicher (ed.), *Berg Encyclopedia of World Dress and Fashion*, vol. 10, Oxford: Berg, pp. 3–10.

Eicher, J. B., Evenson, S. L., and Lutz, H. (eds) (2008), *The Visible Self: Perspectives of Dress, Culture, and Society,* 3rd ed., New York: Fairchild Publishers.

Eicher, J. B., and Roach-Higgins, M. E. (1992), 'Definition and Classification of Dress', in R. Barnes and J. B. Eicher (eds), *Dress and Gender: Making and Meaning in Cultural Context*, Oxford: Berg, pp. 8–17.

El Guindi, F. (1999), *Veil: Modesty, Privacy and Resistance*, Oxford: Berg.

Emmett, A. (2007), 'A Ritual Garment, the Synagogue, and Gender Questions', *Material Religion,* 3/1: 76–87.

Encyclopedia Britannica (2003), Chicago: Encyclopedia Britannica.

Ernst, C. W., and Lawrence, B. (2002), *Sufi Martyrs of Love: The Chishti Order in South Asia and Beyond*, New York: Palgrave Macmillan Netton.

Evans-Wentz, W. Y. (1973 [1927]), *The Tibetan Book of the Dead*, New York: Causeway Books.

Ezzy, D. (2011), 'An Underworld Rite: A Pagan Re-enactment of Persephone's Descent into the Underworld', *Journal of Contemporary Religion*, 26/2: 245–59.

Fabius, C. (1998), *Mehndi: The Art of Henna Body Painting*, New York: Three Rivers Press.

Flood, G. (1996), *An Introduction to Hinduism,* Cambridge: Cambridge University Press.

Flynn, M. (1996), 'The Spiritual Uses of Pain in Spanish Mysticism', *Journal of the American Academy of Religion*, 64/2: 257–78.

Fuchs, R. Y. Y. (1985), *Halichos Bas Yisrael, A Woman's Guide to Jewish Observance,* New York: Feldheim.

Garrett, R. I., with Farrant, R. (2003), *Crossing Over: One Woman's Escape from Amish Life*, San Francisco: Harper.

Goffman, E. (1973), *The Presentation of Self in Everyday Life*, New York: Overlook Press.

González-Wippler, M. (1992), *The Santería Experience: A Journey into the Miraculous*, St. Paul, MN: Llewellyn Publications.

Gordon, B. (1987), 'Fossilized Fashion: Dress as a Symbol of a Separate, Work-oriented Identity', *Dress,* 13: 49–59.

Gordon, L. (2000), *The Book of Voodoo,* Milsons Point, NSW: Random House.

Graybill, B., and Arthur, L. B. (1999), 'The Social Control of Women's Bodies in Two Mennonite Communities', in L. B. Arthur (ed.), *Religion, Dress and the Body*, Oxford: Berg, pp. 9–29.

Hamilton, J. A., and Hawley, J. M. (1999), 'Sacred Dress, Public Worlds: Amish and Mormon Experience and Commitment', in L. B. Arthur (ed.), *Religion, Dress and the Body*, Oxford: Berg, pp. 31–52.

Hartsuiker, D. (1993), *Sadhus: Holy Men of India,* London: Thames and Hudson.

Hausner, S. L. (2007), *Wandering with Sadhus: Ascetics in the Hindu Himalayas,* Bloomington: Indiana University Press.

Hawley, J. S. (ed.) (1994), *Sati: The Blessing and the Curse*, New York: Oxford University Press.

Helminski, C. (2006), 'Sema, the Turning of the Soul', www.sufism.org/society/ articles/sema_camille.html, accessed 7 June 2006.

Hertel, B.R. (2009), 'Hindu Beliefs and Traditions', in C. D. Bryant and D. L. Peck (eds), *Encyclopedia of Death and the Human Experience*, Thousand Oaks, CA: Sage Publications, pp. 561–5.

Hostetler, J.A. (1997), *Hutterite Society*, Baltimore, MD: Johns Hopkins University Press.

Howes, D. (ed.) (2005), *Empire of the Senses: The Sensual Culture Reader*, Oxford: Berg.

Howes, D. (ed.) (2009), *The Sixth Sense Reader*, Oxford: Berg.

Hullet, A., and Roces, A. (1981), 'Thaipusam', *Geo: Australasia's Geographical Magazine*, 3/4: 70–97.

Hume, L. (1988), 'Christianity Full Circle: Aboriginal Christianity on Yarrabah Reserve', in T. Swain and D. B. Rose (eds), *Aboriginal Australians and Christian Missions*, Bedford Park, South Australia: Australian Association for the Study of Religions, pp. 250–62.

Hume, L. (1990), 'Yarrabah: Christian Phoenix: Christianity and Social Change on an Australian Aboriginal Reserve', unpublished PhD thesis, The University of Queensland, Australia.

Hume, L. (1997), *Witchcraft and Paganism in Australia*, Carlton, Victoria: Melbourne University Press.

Hume, L. (2010), 'Ceremonial and Religious Dress in Australia', in J. B. Eicher (ed.), *Berg Encyclopedia of World Dress and Fashion*, vol. 7, Oxford: Berg, pp. 189–94.

Hurbon, L. (1995), *Voodoo: Truth and Fantasy,* London: Thames and Hudson.

Hurst, C.E., and McConnell, D. L. (2010), *An Amish Paradox: Diversity and Change in the World's Largest Amish Community*, Baltimore, MD: Johns Hopkins University Press.

Jaiwent, P. E. (2004), *Banaras and Sarnath,* New Delhi: Roli Books.

Johansen, K. (2010), 'Perfumed Dress and Textiles', in J. B. Eicher (ed.), *Berg Encyclopedia of World Dress and Fashion*, vol. 10, Oxford: Berg, pp. 47–51.

Joseph, N. (1986), *Uniforms and Non-uniforms: Communication Through Clothing*, New York: Greenwood Press.

Karuna, Sr. Canda (2012), 'The Tradition of Buddha's Robe', www.urbandharma.org, accessed 15 April 2012.

Kawlra, A. (2010), 'The Sari', in J. B. Eicher (ed.), *Berg Encyclopedia of World Dress and Fashion*, vol. 4, Oxford: Berg, pp. 115–28.

Kay, S., and Rubin, M. (eds) (1994), *Framing Medieval Bodies,* Manchester: Manchester University Press.

Keenan, W. J. F. (2000), 'Clothed with Authority: The Rationalization of Marist Dress-Culture', in L. B. Arthur (ed.), *Undressing Religion: Commitment and Conversion from a Cross-Cultural Perspective*, Oxford: Berg, pp. 83–100.

Kendall, L. (1985), *Shamans, Housewives, and Other Restless Spirits,* Honolulu: University of Hawaii.

Kennett, F., with MacDonald-Haig, C. (1994), *World Dress*, London: Mitchell Beazley.

Khuri, F. I. (2001), *The Body in Islamic Culture*, London: Saqi Books.

Kister, D. (2004), 'Korean Shamanism', in M. N. Walter and E. J. N. Fridman (eds), *Shamanism: An Encyclopedia of World Beliefs, Practices, and Culture,* vol. 2, Santa Barbara, CA: ABC-CLIO, pp. 681–8.

Ki Tov, E. (1963), *The Jew and His Home*, New York: Shengold Publishers.

Knauft, B. M. (1989), 'Bodily Images in Melanesia: Cultural Substances and Natural Metaphors', in M. Feher, with R. Naddaff and N. Tazi (eds), *Fragments for a History of the Human Body*, part 3, New York: Zone, pp. 199–258.

Kramer, K. P. (1988), *The Sacred Art of Dying: How World Religions Understand Death*, New York: Paulist Press.

Kraybill, D. B. (2008), *The Amish of Lancaster County*, Mechanicsburg, PA: Stackpole Books.

Kuhns, E. (2003), *The Habit: A History of the Clothing of Catholic Nuns,* New York: Doubleday.

Landman, I. (ed.) (2009), *The Universal Jewish Encyclopedia*, New York: The Universal Jewish Encyclopedia Inc.

Litten, J. (1991), *The English Way of Death: The Common Funeral since 1450,* London: Robert Hale.

Littrell, M. A., and Ogle, J. P. (2007), 'Women, Migration, and the Experience of Dress', in D. C. Johnson and H. B. Foster (eds), *Dress Sense*, Oxford: Berg, pp. 121–32.

Lommel, A. (1967), *Shamanism: The Beginnings of Art,* New York: McGraw-Hill.

Longridge, W. H. (trans.) (1919), *The Spiritual Exercises of Saint Ignatius of Loyola*, London: Robert Scott Roxburghe House Paternoster Rows, EC.

Maginnis, T. (2004), 'Costume, Shaman', in M. N. Walter and E. J. N. Fridman (eds), *Shamanism: An Encyclopedia of World Beliefs, Practices, and Culture*, vol. 1, Santa Barbara, CA: ABC-CLIO, pp. 57–61.

Maher, M. (2006), *Judaism*, Blackrock, County Dublin: Columba Press.

Maynard, M. (2004), *Dress and Globalisation,* Manchester: Manchester University Press.

McLay, A. (1996), *Women on the Move: Mercy's Triple Spiral,* Adelaide, South Australia: Sisters of Mercy.

McLeod, W. H. (1989), *The Sikhs: History, Religion, and Society,* New York: Columbia University Press.

Melton, J. G., and Baumann, M. (eds) (2002), *Religions of the World: A Comprehensive Encyclopedia of Beliefs and Practices*, Santa Barbara, CA: ABC-CLIO.

Mernissi, F. (1994), *The Harem Within: Tales of a Moroccan Girlhood*, Toronto: Bantam Books.

Murphy, J. M. (1994), *Working the Spirit: Ceremonies of the African Diaspora*, Boston: Beacon Press.

Netton, I. R. (2000), *Sufi Ritual: The Parallel Universe,* Richmond, Surrey: Curzon Press.

Neusner, J., Avery-Peck, A. J., and Green, W. S. (eds) (2000), *Encyclopedia of Judaism*, Leiden and Boston, MA: Brill.

Ó Murchú, D. (2000), *Religion in Exile: A Spiritual Vision for the Homeward Bound*, Dublin: Gill and Macmillan.

Ouaknin, M.-A. (1997 [1995]), *Symbols of Judaism*, Paris: Editions Assouline.

Oxford Dictionary of Buddhism (2004), Oxford: Oxford University Press.

Pérez y Mena, A. I. (1998), 'Cuban Santería, Haitian Vodun, Puerto Rican Spiritualism: A Multicultural Inquiry into Syncretism', *Journal for the Scientific Study of Religion,* 37/1: 15–27.

Pérez y Mena, A. I. (1999), 'Santería', in W. C. Roof (ed.), *Contemporary American Religion,* New York: Macmillan.

Pike, S. (2001), *Earthly Bodies, Magical Selves: Contemporary Pagans and the Search for Community*, Berkeley: University of California.

Potapov, L. P. (1999), 'Shaman's Drum: A Unique Monument of Spiritual Culture of the Altai Turk Peoples', *Anthropology of Consciousness,* 10/4: 24–35.

Rabten, G. (2000), *The Life of a Tibetan Monk: Autobiography of a Tibetan Meditation Master*, Le Mont-Pèlerin: Edition Rabten.

Renne, E. P. (2000), 'Cloth and Conversion: Yoruba Textiles and Ecclesiastical Dress', in L. B. Arthur (ed.), *Undressing Religion: Commitment and Conversion from a Cross-Cultural Perspective*, Oxford: Berg, pp. 7–24.

Ribeiro, A. (2003 [1986]), *Dress and Morality*, Oxford: Berg.

Rinpoche, Lama Z. (2005), 'Sangha Dress Code', *Sangha Magazine* (September): 20–2.

Shirazi, F. (2000), 'Islamic Religion and Women's Dress Code: The Islamic Republic of Iran', in L. B. Arthur (ed.), *Undressing Religion: Commitment and Conversion from a Cross-Cultural Perspective*, Oxford: Berg, pp. 113–30.

Shirey, H. (2012), 'Candomblé Beads and Identity in Salvador da Bahia, Brazil', *Nova Religio*, 16: 36–60.

Shukla, P. (2008), *The Grace of Four Moons: Dress, Adornment, and the Art of the Body in Modern India*, Bloomington: Indiana University Press.

Silverman, E. (2013), *A Cultural History of Jewish Dress*, London: Bloomsbury.

Singh, J. (2010), 'Head First: Young British Sikhs, Hair, and the Turban', *Journal of Contemporary Religion*, 25/2: 203–20.

Singh, N.-G. K. (2004), 'Sacred Fabric and Sacred Stitches: The Underwear of the Khalsa', *History of Religions*, 43/4: 284–302.

Sisters of Mercy, Brisbane (2004), *Our Spiral Dance: Past, Present and Future* [CD-ROM], Adelaide, South Australia: Sisters of Mercy.

Smart, N. (1989), *The World's Religions,* Cambridge: Cambridge University Press.

Sopa, G. L. (2007/2008), 'Tibetan Monastic Robes', *Mandala* (December/January): 48–50.

Steele, P. (2005), *The Medieval World*, New York: Facts on File.

Swain, T., and Rose, D. B. (eds) (1988), *Aboriginal Australians and Christian Missions*, Bedford Park, South Australia: Australian Association for the Study of Religions.

Swatos, W. H. Jr. (ed.) (1998), *Encyclopedia of Religion and Society,* Walnut Creek, CA: Altamira Press.

Sweet, M. J. (trans.) (2010), *Mission to Tibet: The Extraordinary Eighteenth-Century Account of Father Ippolito Desideri, S. J.*, ed. L. Zwilling, Boston: Wisdom Publications.

Tanabe, W. J. (2003), 'Robes and Clothing', in R. E. Buswell, Jr. (ed.), *Encyclopedia of Buddhism*, vol. 2, New York: Macmillan Reference, pp. 731–5.

Tarlo, E. (2010), *Visibly Muslim: Fashion, Politics, Faith*, Oxford: Berg.

Taylor, L. (2009), *Mourning Dress: A Costume and Social History,* Abingdon, Oxon: Routledge.

Thieme, O. C., and Eicher, J. B. (1990), 'African Dress: Form, Action, Meaning', in B. Starke, L. O. Holloman and B. Nordquist (eds), *African American Dress and Adornment: A Cultural Perspective*, Dubuque, IA: Kendall Hunt, pp. 69–80.

Thurman, R.A.F. (1995), *Inside Tibetan Buddhism*, San Francisco: Collins Publishers.

Tortora, P. (2010), 'Religion and Dress', in J.B. Eicher (ed.), *Berg Encyclopedia of World Dress and Fashion*, vol. 3, Oxford: Berg, pp. 486–90.

Townsend, J. B. (1997), 'Shamanism', in S. Glazier (ed.) *Anthropology of Religion: A Handbook,* Westport, CT: Greenwood.

Townsend, J. B. (2004), 'Core Shamanism and Neo-Shamanism' in M. N. Walter and E. J. N. Fridman (eds), *Shamanism: An Encyclopedia of World Beliefs, Practices, and Culture,* vol. 1, Santa Barbara, CA: ABC-CLIO, pp. 49–56.

Tselos, S. (2000), 'Dressing the Divine Horsemen: Clothing as Spirit Identification in Haitian Vodou', in L.B. Arthur (ed.), *Undressing Religion: Commitment and Conversion from a Cross-Cultural Perspective*, Oxford: Berg, pp. 45–64.

Tselos, S. (2010), 'Vodou Ritual Garments in Haiti', in J. B. Eicher (ed.), *Berg Encyclopedia of World Dress and Fashion*, vol. 2, Oxford: Berg, pp. 252–6.

Turner, B. (1984), *Body and Society*, Oxford: Basil Blackwell.

Turner, T. (1980), 'The Social Skin', in J. Cherfas and R. Lewin (eds), *Not Work Alone: A Cross-Cultural View of Activities Superfluous to Survival*, Beverly Hills, CA: Sage Publications, pp. 112–39.

Valiente, D. (1978), *Witchcraft for Tomorrow*, Custer, WA: Phoenix.

Vallely, A. (2009), 'Jainism', in P. B. Clarke and P. Beyer (eds), *The World's Religions: Continuities and Transformations*, London: Routledge, pp. 325–37.

Van Gennep, A. (1960), *The Rites of Passage*, Chicago: University of Chicago Press.

Vitebsky, P. (2001), *The Shaman*, London: Duncan Baird Publishers.

Vogelsang-Eastwood, G. (2010), 'Snapshot: Islamic Pilgrimage Dress', in J.B. Eicher (ed.), *Berg Encyclopedia of World Dress and Fashion*, vol. 5, Oxford: Berg, pp. 443–5.

Wafer, J. (1991), *The Taste of Blood: Spirit Possession in Brazilian Candomblé*, Philadelphia: University of Pennsylvania Press.

Walter, M. N., and Fridman, E. J. N. (eds) (2004), *Shamanism: An Encyclopedia of World Beliefs, Practices, and Culture,* 2 vols, Santa Barbara, CA: ABC-CLIO.

Wikkan, U. (1982), *Behind the Veil in Arabia: Women in Oman,* Chicago: University of Chicago Press.

Wogan-Browne, J. (1994), 'Chaste Bodies: Frames and Experiences', in S. Kay and M. Rubin (eds), *Framing Medieval Bodies*, Manchester: Manchester University Press, pp. 24–42.

Wolff, N. H. (2004), 'Yoruba', in C. R. Ember and M. Ember (eds), *Encyclopedia of Medical Anthropology: Health and Illness in the World's Cultures*, vol. 2, New York: Springer, pp. 1029–39.

WEBSITES

www.BuddhaNet

www.ahimsasilks.com

www.bbc.co.uk/religion/religions/candomble

www.bbc.co.uk/religion/religions/sikhism/customs/fiveks.shtml

www.bbc.co.uk/religion/religions/hinduism

www.dlshq.org/religions/jainism.htm

www.jewfaq.org/signs.htm

www.newadvent.org/cathen/10190b.htm

www.geovision.com.my/malaysia/general/religious/festivals/thaipusam.html

www.history.mennonite.net/

www.hutteriteheritage.com

www.hutteriteheritage.com

www.hutterites.org/religion.htm

www.jainism.org

www.jewfaq.org/signs.htm

www.jewishvirtuallibrary.org/jsource/Judaism/Kippah.html

www.sadhus.org/

www.sikhnet.com/s/WhyTurbans

www.sikhs.org/

www.sufism/org/society/sema2.html

www.thecanadianencyclopedia.com

www.thehijabshop.com

http://utopia.knoware.l.users/dolfhart/sects.html

www.whirlingdervishes.org/whirlingdervishes.htm

www.wildfilmsindia.com

www2.etown.edu/amishstudies/Population_Trends_2012.asp

Index